GOD, A BOY AND World War II

by Karl Feucht

God, A Boy and World War II

I dedicate this story to

ANDREW LANDRITH

and to all the boys at Hillcrest Children's Home

in Hot Springs, Arkansas.

It was at Andrew's request for my war story that I even considered writing it, and when several other boys also asked for it, I sat down and began putting it together. They waited long and patiently until I finally got it all done. Thank you fellas for being so patient with me. You all are truly a great bunch of guys. I hope you will like and enjoy this story and that it will be a blessing to each one of you. I pray that it will help you in your own lives to be what God wants you to be.

God bless each and every one of you!!

TABLE OF CONTENTS

PROLOGUE

May 21, 1943

There we stood, on the auditorium platform, nine boys and eight girls, in our caps and gowns, clutching in our hand what we had worked twelve long years to receive...our DIPLOMAS!! It's hard to describe exactly how we felt...especially the guys. Sure, we were glad that school days were over, but now we faced a very uncertain future—the Military and War. Of the nine of us boys, eight of us went into the service. One was rejected because of a heart condition. He was killed in a car accident just after the war ended—a week after he had gotten married! Only one of the eight of us that went into the service never came home. As of today, February 2004, four of us are still living.

High School Graduation
June 21, 1943
Age 18

I

IN THE BEGINNING

It was a bright sunny day in early June of 1943, as I stood in front of our mailbox. In my hand I held the letter I had been expecting—yet dreading—the letter from Uncle Sam. With mixed emotions, I read that I was to report to Columbus, Ohio, on June 21, 1943, for examination and induction into military service and then to Fort Benjamin Harrison, Indiana, for active duty July 6, 1943. I had been "selected" by Uncle Sam—so the letter stated!! I stood staring at the letter for some time, my thoughts all mixed up and my mind in a whirl. I had just turned eighteen in April and had graduated from High School in May. Although I knew that our little farm of sixteen acres wasn't enough to keep me out of the service, I prayed that somehow God would work things out so I wouldn't have to go. NOW, here I stood with my orders in my hand. Besides, I had never been away from home except for overnight stays with my grandparents and a one week stay with a buddy of mine from church who lived on a large dairy farm about fifteen miles from our house.

Slowly, I made my way up the lane, dreading to break the news to my Mom and Dad. I knew my Mom would take it hard. I wasn't sure about my Dad since he and I weren't getting along very well. I really loved my Dad, but there just were so many things we didn't agree on, causing a lot of conflict and bad feelings. I had seriously thought about running away from home when I was fourteen, but I didn't. Now, I HAD to leave and I didn't want to!!

It's hard to describe my feelings as we drove the sixteen miles to the train station in Dayton. I dreaded saying "good-bye" because I knew that Mom would cry, and I was having a hard enough time to keep from doing that myself!!

Since my orders said that I had to have a "regulation Army" haircut, we stopped on the way to get my hair cut. A "regulation Army" haircut is 1½ inches long, but I don't think that barber had the foggiest idea of what an Army haircut was. When he finished, there wasn't a hair on my head over 1/8 of an inch long!! HE must have been in the Navy!! I looked downright horrible!! I was so mad I could have croaked him on the spot!! When I got to the train station, I really got mad. Practically all of the fifty or more guys going to Columbus too, had NOT gotten haircuts at all, and their hair was definitely longer than 1½ inches!! To top it off, NOT a word was said about hair or haircuts after we arrived at the Induction Center in

Columbus. For months afterwards, I would not let ANY barber touch the top of my head until my hair had grown out again—completely!!

Upon our arrival in Columbus late that afternoon, we were taken to a hotel for the night with instructions to be ready at eight o'clock the next morning when we would be taken to the Induction Center. At the Center the next morning, we were given a basket for our clothes and ordered to strip down completely! For the rest of that day, we went from one examination and test to another in our birthday suits!! All that day, I was punched, poked, jabbed, thumped, banged on and looked into—and finally passed as a healthy human being—fit to go out and get shot!!

As we stood in line waiting to find out what branch of the service we would be in, the boy in front of me and I got to talking. I found out that he too did not want to be in the Navy. We had heard that when a guy got into the Navy and they found out that he couldn't swim, they would throw him into the water and make him learn how to swim. (We found out later that that wasn't completely true. It was just one of those rumors to scare new guys who were just coming into the service.) Since neither of us knew how to swim, we were scared! When the guy in front of the one I was talking to got to the desk, the officer didn't ask him what branch of the service he wanted; instead, he asked, "Do you like water?"

A bit surprised, the boy stammered, "Well...y-yes."

"Okay, you're in the Navy," the officer snapped as he stamped the boy's papers. As the boy tried to protest, the officer ordered him to move on, while our hearts sank down to our feet! Now, it was my friend's turn. He was quickly assigned to the Army—much to his relief. I was still holding my breath and praying when I stepped up to the desk.

"What branch of the service do you prefer?" the officer asked. I had prayed for the Lord's will to be done, and now, it was in His hands.

"A-Army," I stammered. NOW I was really holding my breath!!

I let it all out with a big "whoosh" when I heard him say, "Okay, Army it is," stamping "ARMY" on my papers as he spoke.

At that moment I didn't realize that God had already begun working out His plans for my life. I was still thickheaded, wondering WHY He hadn't answered my prayers and kept me out of the service...PERIOD! NOW, here I was going into the ARMY!

That afternoon I raised my right hand and was sworn in as a member of the U.S. Army. I was now a soldier and the property of UNCLE SAM!!

My first orders came the next day. I was to return home, wind up all my personal affairs and report for active duty at Fort Benjamin Harrison, Indiana, on the 6th of July. That gave me two weeks at home.

II
ACTIVE DUTY

After two weeks of many "good-byes," I arrived in Fort Benjamin Harrison along with several hundred other men. Here, we received our uniform and equipment and were assigned to our basic training camp. Again, God was working for me, but I was too full of my own feelings to realize it. As I stepped up to the officer making the assignments, he asked, "Do you have any objections to taking up arms and taking another man's life?…" and he rattled off a long list of other things.

I interrupted him and said, "Yes."

"Yes…what?" he asked.

"To taking up arms and taking another man's life," I answered.

"Do you have any proof or anything to back you up?"

"Yes," I replied, as I handed him the letter and papers I had received from the Assemblies of God headquarters in Springfield, Missouri.

After looking them over thoroughly, he handed them back to me saying, "Okay—everything seems to be in order."

He then proceeded to print information in big red letters on the outside of my records. I was then assigned to the U.S. Army Medical Department and shipped off to Camp Grant, Illinois, a medical training camp ninety miles west of Chicago. This was to be my home until the end of October, and it was the beginning of living in tents.

I soon discovered the meaning of "fast foods"!! We were allowed fifteen minutes from the time we entered the mess hall to get our tray, go through the line for our food, find a place to sit down and then eat...BEFORE the fifteen minutes expired!! A Sergeant walked up and down the aisle, and when HE thought your time was up...you left whether you were finished or not.

Camp Grant, Illinois

July, 1943

We usually didn't wait for him to tell us! Eating that Army chow that fast, three meals a day, seven days a week, sure didn't do our stomachs any good, and many of us wound up with stomach problems later. We were surprised when we saw plates instead of trays, but after the first few times through the chow line, when we saw how the food was plopped on our plates, we wanted the trays with the dividers. It seemed that the guys serving the food took special delight in piling the food on your plate—one thing on top of the other. The dessert, which was usually Jell-O, was plopped on top of everything else! What a mess! (Maybe that's why they called our meals "mess" and the dining room the "mess hall"!!!) We griped and complained, although we doubted that it would do any good. However, it must have finally gotten through to someone, because two weeks later, we came into the mess hall, and lo and behold, there were shiny new trays with dividers!! What an improvement!! Even then some of the servers couldn't hit one of sections, but we didn't complain because if we did, they would miss the section deliberately. Oh well, at least our Jell-O was separate, most of the time!!

For the next three months, our daily routine was calisthenics, classes, long hikes night and day, bivouacs, obstacle courses with live ammunition fired just above our heads and simulated battles where we practiced bandaging imaginary wounds and injuries. We were training to be First Aid Corpsmen on the front lines.

The one bright spot during all this time was that on Saturday afternoons, after our games, which we HAD to attend, we were able to get a weekend pass. I would always have my suitcase ready, and the minute the "games" were over and we were free, I got my pass as quickly as I could and made a bee-line for the train to Chicago where I changed trains for Dayton and arrived home early Sunday morning. I left again late Sunday evening, getting back to camp just before the midnight deadline. It wasn't a long time to spend at home, but it was HOME, and Mom's fried chicken was worth the trip!!

As our basic training was nearing the end, we were marched one day to the Dispensary for our final series of shots. We were to get two shots, one in each arm, and a small-pox vaccination. As we entered the Dispensary, we saw two medics, one on each side of our line. As each man stepped in between them, he got stuck in each arm at the same time. Getting stuck was bad enough, but the two medics doing the sticking were JAPANESE!! We could hardly believe our eyes!! They saw the looks on our faces and heard some of the comments being made and were really amused. THEY were really getting a kick out of it. Since they were Japanese-Americans and were in the Army too, (OUR Army), everything turned out O.K. I guess it was better getting "shot" with needles by Japanese-Americans, than "shot" with bullets by Japanese soldiers! After they got through with us, we passed on to the next stop, with an American, and got our small-pox vaccination. When that was done, we went out the rear door of the Dispensary, around to the front where we fell into formation to march back to our quarters. All of a sudden things started spinning around and getting black. If I hadn't dropped to the ground and laid down right then, I would have passed out completely. I was really embarrassed. I had never had shots affect me like that before.

I was even more embarrassed when the Corporal in charge hollered, "What's the matter Feucht, can't you take it?" I could tell by his voice that he wasn't being sarcastic. "Take it easy and when you can, go to the nearest latrine (rest room), wash your face in cold water and come on back to your tent as soon as you can."

With that, he marched the platoon back to our quarters, and I eventually made it back myself. I found out afterwards that I wasn't the only one who almost passed out—there were a lot of others who passed out completely. I don't know if it was all the shots—or the idea of getting "shot" by Japanese-Americans—or both!!

I'll never forget the boy we had in camp who had never worn shoes before he got into the Army. He was so excited. He went all around camp showing everybody his "new" shoes.

"Look at my new shoes," he beamed. "Ain't they purrty?"

I never thought of Army shoes as being "purrty," but HE sure thought they were!!

Then, there was the guy who had never seen snow. Toward the end of October, the weather began threatening to snow. A lot of us who were used to the winters in the North were saying that it might snow anytime because it sure looked like it was going to.

"Will you guys shut up already!" he exploded one day. "I've never seen snow, and you guys are scaring me!"

He really was scared. The poor guy didn't know WHAT to expect—he didn't have the slightest idea how snow came!! I don't know if he ever found out because we were shipped out before it did snow.

All this time I was praying that I would not have to go overseas, but IF I did have to go overseas, I prayed that I wouldn't have to go to the Pacific area of the war. I did not want to go overseas at all (who did?) but I most definitely preferred Europe over Japan—even though I had several uncles in the German Army.

Finally, in the last week of October, our basic training completed, we received our orders—sealed orders, which we were not to open until we were on the train and on our way. The suspense was awful; we had no idea where we were headed. We could hardly wait!!

While the man in charge of our group of seven men opened the envelope, we were all standing around him holding our breath. Until then, we had determined that our train was heading west, which gave us a sinking feeling. Japan was in the West. Our destination was Barnes General Hospital in Vancouver, Washington—on the West Coast! My heart sank because when you were shipped to the West Coast, it meant that you were headed for the Pacific War Zone. Bitterly, I cried, "Again, Lord, You have not answered my prayers...WHY??" I really felt that the Lord had deserted me, forgetting His promise "never to leave me or forsake me." But, the

Lord knew what He was doing. He had His plans for me, and I just needed to yield my will and myself to Him. I had to be willing to follow wherever He wanted to lead me.

III
ON THE WEST COAST: VANCOUVER AND PORTLAND

When we arrived in Vancouver, it was cold and raining. For all of us, this was our first visit to the Pacific Northwest: very beautiful country but WET!! Barnes General Hospital was a large "solid" hospital—no tents. How good it felt to live and sleep in a real building again, even if they were wooden barracks! In basic training, we had been trained under battle conditions as First Aid Men, now we were to receive hospital training working with real patients. However, they were not men wounded in battle. It was good training and experience. It was the first time I ever changed a whole bed with someone in it!! Unknown to us at the time, the seven of us were brought together with doctors, nurses and other personnel from all over the States to form a new General Hospital. I was now a member of the 76th General Hospital…and would be until the war was over. The question was WHERE were we going from here???

Vancouver was not a large city; consequently there wasn't a whole lot of to do there. Whenever we got passes, we all went across the Columbia River to Portland, Oregon. Being a much larger city, there was much more to do and see. Every Saturday afternoon, there was a mad rush to the bus station to catch the bus for Portland. My first weekend in Portland was one I will never forget. I had gone to Portland hoping to find a church to go to Sunday morning. When I finally located the United Service Organization (U.S.O.), I immediately reserved a bed for the night. This was the only place to go, since I didn't know anyone in Portland. Then I went to the desk and got a listing of all the churches. I found several Assemblies of God churches listed, but since I had no idea where they were located, I just picked one and figured I'd find out how to get to it later. I had no idea just how God's hand was directing my steps and my life.

I left the U.S.O to find a restaurant. I was hungry!! As I stood on a corner in downtown Portland waiting for the traffic light to change, a little, short man approached me and handed me a gospel tract. I started to stick it into my pocket when I noticed the name of a church stamped on the back. It was an Assemblies of God church!! I turned and quickly found the man who had given me the tract.

After giving me directions to the church in some detail he said, "Our Pastor and young people from the church will be holding a street meeting on this corner at seven o'clock, why don't you come?"

"I'm going to get something to eat now, but I'll be there," I told him with a good feeling in my heart. Things were really turning out okay.

At seven o'clock, I was back on that corner just in time for the meeting. Everyone in the group was very friendly—making this lonely soldier boy welcome. There was one lady who drew my attention. She was attractive, but that wasn't what drew my attention to her; I already had a girlfriend back home, so I wasn't looking for a girl. Besides, this lady was older than me. It was the love of Jesus shining from her face and eyes that drew me. After the meeting I had a nice chat with her and discovered that she had four sisters at home—the youngest one close to my age. If I came to church in the morning, she informed me, I would meet them all and her parents, too. After telling her that I had already planned to be there, I left that street corner with a warm feeling in my heart. I had found some friends on my first day in Portland!!

Early Sunday morning, after a quick breakfast, I walked to 12th and Taylor where the Portland Gospel Tabernacle was supposed to be. Instead, I found a large Baptist Church on one corner. I quickly checked the tract with the church's address on it and checked the street signs and realized that I was on <u>S.W.</u> 12th and Taylor. The church I was looking for was on <u>S.E.</u> 12th and Taylor—clear on the other side of the Willamette River—on the opposite side of the city!! I quickly found a streetcar that took me across the river within a few blocks of the right church! I arrived just as the service was about to start.

After the service and many welcomes, I met my friend from the street meeting and her family, including her youngest sister, Margaret. I also met a couple with two small boys, Douglas and Ronald, who invited me to their home for dinner and for the rest of the day. This was the beginning of a beautiful friendship, and from that day on, I spent many pleasant and enjoyable hours in that home. I came on Saturday afternoon, stayed overnight and attended church with them on Sunday. In fact, anytime I could wrangle a pass, I was in the home of my friends. I was concerned that maybe I was coming too much, and that I was being a bother, but they wouldn't hear of it. Imagine my surprise when I discovered that my friend from the street meeting and her family lived right next door!!

As it turned out, Margaret came over and visited several times while I was there. (I didn't know that my friend, trying to play Cupid, had invited her over!) I admired her because of her love for Jesus, and I really enjoyed her company, but since I had a girl back home that was as far as it went. She understood and respected that. I was so impressed with her that one day after she left, I told my friend that Margaret sure was a wonderful Christian girl and that they guy who got her for his wife would really be a fortunate and blessed fellow!! Little did I realize how the hand of God was moving in my life! I was still "upset" with God for not answering my prayers. So I thought! After all, wasn't I here on the West Coast headed for the Pacific War Zone??

I guess you could say that those times were the bright and pleasant part of our days in Vancouver. The work at the hospital wasn't really hard—just boring and monotonous. Changing beds, mopping and waxing floors, polishing everything that could be polished and any other clean-up jobs, including messes made by patients didn't exactly make for a pleasant day, especially six days a week, week after week. Our care of the patients consisted mainly of fetching bedpans and urinals. We never dressed any wounds, changed bandages or gave shots or injections of any kind. Some of the guys began to complain.

"We thought we were supposed to be training to be medics or Corpsmen…NOT janitors!!!"

One day, in an effort to break the monotony, my co-worker and I started having a water fight. We were washing and sterilizing syringes. When we filled them with water, they made ideal weapons! I had a large syringe full of water aimed directly at my buddy's head. Just as I gave the plunger a hard push, he jumped to one side, and the head nurse on our ward, who had just stepped into the doorway, got the full benefit of my "shot" directly in her face!!

"Okay, you guys," she sputtered, "you've had your fun."

"You," she said pointing at me, since I was the one who gave her the shower. "Just for that, YOU can come with me and help me change the dressings!!"

WOW!! Just what I wanted!! She thought she was punishing me! Actually, she was helping me! From that day on, I assisted her with changing dressings. Of course, I apologized for squirting water in her face. I don't know what ever happened to my buddy!

****

The day we dreaded finally arrived when our orders came through, and we knew that we were going overseas. After saying sad good-byes to all our friends, we boarded a train on February 14th—

Valentine's Day. We figured that we were headed for San Francisco

or Los Angeles, which were Ports of Embarkation to the Pacific War

Zone, but we were in for a surprise! Imagine our feelings when we

realized that we were not going South…but EAST!! We lived and ate

on that troop train for seven days, stopping only in wide-open spaces.

That was the only time we were allowed to get off the train and only

for calisthenics. One day, as the train passed through a small town in

Iowa, we saw a woman in her backyard hanging up her laundry.

Suddenly, one of the guys jumped up yelling, "Hey, that's my Mom!"

It was all we could do to keep him from jumping off that train. In

fact, some of the guys held him until we were well past that yard and

town.

On the seventh day, we arrived in Camp Miles Standish, a

short distance from Boston, Massachusetts. There was no doubt now

where we were headed. For two weeks, we were given our Medical

Department Identification Cards. As long as we carried that card, we

were not allowed to carry weapons of any kind. If we went on guard

duty, which required carrying a rifle, we had to turn the card in to the

office until we came off guard duty: that was according to the Rules of the Geneva Convention agreed to by all the Nations after World War I. At the end of two weeks, we were back on the train, bound for Boston Harbor and our ship. There could not have been a more angry, dejected and confused boy as I was as I walked up that gangplank onto that ship. I had prayed, but my prayers were not answered. WHY wasn't HE hearing me? I was sure that the Lord had forgotten all about me!!

As we sailed out of Boston Harbor, we met a large fleet of ships and found ourselves smack in the middle of one of the largest convoys to ever cross the Atlantic Ocean up to that time. Each ship was assigned its own position and the whole convoy maintained the speed of the slowest ship in the convoy. If a ship broke down and was unable to make quick repairs, it was left behind. They could not endanger the rest of the convoy for one ship. For the first six days, several U.S. Navy Destroyers continually circled the convoy, protecting it from enemy submarines. On the seventh day, they returned to the U.S., and we were on our own!!

S.S. "GEORGE WASHINGTON."

LENGTH 722. BREADTH 78. DEPTH 52. REGISTERED TONNAGE 27,000.

Former -- German Liner ~ "S.S. Dresden" Built in 1907. This Took Me To War!

The ship we were on was the U.S. ARMY TRANSPORT "George Washington," a former German luxury liner. It was a large ship, but because there were over 2,000 troops on board representing many different outfits, we were restricted to the part of the ship we were in. We were required to wear a life jacket constantly, the exception being at night when we used it for a pillow. Woe to the man who was caught without his life jacket! Some of the guys slept with it on, but I found them so uncomfortable during the day, I wasn't about to wear the miserable thing at night if I didn't have to!! There was a store, or PX, where we could buy cigarettes, candy bars, cans of peanuts, fig newtons and other things at bargain prices. I was only interested in the things you could eat, and I ate so many peanuts and fig newtons, it's a wonder I didn't sink the ship! Although our meals were okay for Army chow, I was munching peanuts and fig newtons all day long. I wasn't the only one either since there just wasn't anything else to do. The only time we stopped was when we had life boat drills. IF the Nazis didn't sink our ship, THIS was our "home" for fourteen days.

Being only eighteen, I didn't have much of a beard yet, but I did shave occasionally. However, after the first shave, I limited my shaving to as few times as possible and took only ONE shower while on that ship. If you've never shaved or taken a shower in cold, salty ocean water, you have really missed something!! Try it sometime!! It is absolutely impossible to get any suds or foam when you soap yourself. It's like smearing grease all over your body. As for shaving, forget the shaving cream! It worked no better than soap. When I finished shaving, my face felt like I had used sandpaper. All THAT just to scrape off a little fuzz!! You can be sure that we were a pretty smelly bunch when we got off that ship, because I wasn't the only one who wouldn't take a shower!!

It was a cold, windy, dreary day when we arrived in Liverpool, England. Solid ground sure felt good under my feet again! We were promptly herded onto a train for a five-hour ride to Llandudno, Wales, on the northern coast of Wales. British trains definitely are NOT like American trains! At least NOT the ones we were on!! Instead of rows of seats on each side with an aisle down the middle, their trains have compartments, which extend from one side to the other with two long benches facing each other. Once you are in that compartment, that's it: you can't go anywhere! What's worse, there are no restrooms!! We hadn't been on that train very long when some of us needed a restroom. Hoping that we wouldn't be on the train very long, we held off as long as we could, but when ya gotta go—ya gotta go!! We finally resorted to using any containers we could find—even our helmets as a last resort—and dumping the contents out the window. One of the guys disgustedly said, "Phooey on that business," and promptly stood up to the window and did what he had to do! The trouble with that was that just at that moment, the train was going around a sharp curve and people in the front part of the train could look back and see the rest of the train. WE were at the BACK of the train, and in the cars ahead of us were our NURSES!! Need I say more?? None of the rest of us even thought of using that window in THAT way!! NO WAY!!

Llandudno was the home of Carroll Lewis who wrote the children's story "Alice in Wonderland." This was only a stopover, not our final destination. We were scattered around the city, living in apartments and buildings taken over by the U.S. Army for billets. For our meals, we had to walk three times a day to our mess hall located in the main part of the city. In my case, this meant a two-mile walk, round trip each time! Good way to work up an appetite, huh? Needless to say, many of us skipped meals quite often. It was much easier to go to a nearby "Fish and Chips" shop and buy some deep-fried fish and chips (that's what the English call French fries). They tasted a lot better than Army chow anyway!!

We were able to do some sightseeing, but our main activity each day was marching and drilling on the "Promenade," a long concrete strip along the beach. There we were, dressed as warm as possible in heavy overcoats and gloves, marching back and forth in a cold, icy March wind blowing in off the ocean—thanks to some smart-aleck officer who wanted to show his authority—and stupidity. We didn't notice HIM out there marching with us!! Down the beach a short distance from us, people (or were they polar bears with swimsuits on??) were SWIMMING in the ocean as if it were summertime!! We wondered WHO was the nuttiest—the swimmers or the bundled up marchers???

One whole month of this kind of living was enough! Believe me, we were very ready to leave Llandudno! This move took us back to England to the town of Leominster (pronounced Lem-inster), where a hospital had been constructed. Now, we knew why we had been sitting in Llandudno for a whole month. We had been waiting for the hospital to be completed, although there was still plenty of work to do after we got there. It was a very busy time for awhile, getting the hospital ready to receive patients, setting up all the surgical and medical equipment and getting it all in proper working order. At least we had good solid buildings. I'm sure that if we had known what lay ahead of us, we would have enjoyed and appreciated it there a lot more.

One afternoon, having some free time, I went into the chapel to relax and play the piano. No one was there, so I had the chapel all to myself. I had been playing for awhile when the chaplain came in from his office to see who was playing. As we talked, he told me that he was having problems with his assistant, who was not a Christian and who had drinking problems, returning from town drunk on numerous occasions.

"Would there be any chance that I could be your assistant?" I asked hopefully.

"Yes, I think so," he replied. "If you are really interested."

"I AM, chaplain, I definitely am," I answered. I wasn't about to let this opportunity slip away.

"Okay," he answered. "I'll work on it. It may take a couple of days but I'll do what I can."

I left the chapel praying that God would work things out so that I could become the chaplain's assistant, not realizing that it was the Lord Who had put it into my heart to go into the chapel at just THAT particular time. Within two days, I was the new chaplain's assistant and was given a desk of my own in the chaplain's office. I was no longer an orderly in a ward taking care of patients. I was now a clerk-typist, assisting the chaplain in all services, keeping records and handling all correspondence. In emergencies or when there was a large amount of wounded coming in, I was still called on to help transport the wounded or help in the wards, although this didn't happen often.

God was still working in my life and had been all along; I just didn't have enough sense to know it!! I was wanting HIM to work things the way I wanted them, but HE knew the plans He had for me and my life. I just needed to let him have HIS way, which, after all is said and done, is the BEST way.

IV
D-DAY: JUNE 6, 1944

On the morning of June 6th, 1944, hereafter to be known as "D-Day," I was in the office and had just turned on the small radio the chaplain had in his office. The program of classical music I was listening to was suddenly interrupted with an announcement, "Early this morning Allied Forces landed on the northern coasts of France. Fierce fighting is now under way." Then General Dwight D. Eisenhower, Supreme Commander of all the Allied Forces, spoke giving encouragement to all the troops involved. Imagine our amazement when in mid-afternoon, we were notified that wounded men from the landings were arriving at our hospital! Boy, they sure weren't wasting any time! From that day on until the day we left Leominster, the wounded came in steadily growing numbers. These were different from the patients we had taken care of back in the States. THIS was no practice! THIS was the REAL thing!! Men with an arm or leg blown off, some with half their faces blown away; all severely wounded in some way. It was amazing that many of them were still alive. In spite of our training, we were not prepared for what we saw. It was heartbreaking and a real shock to many of us— just a foretaste of what was to come.

It didn't take us long to settle down into a regular routine. However, we should have known that it was too good to last. In the middle of July, we packed up all our personal belongings, turned the hospital over to another outfit, climbed onto another train and were on our way to the Port of Southampton where a ship was waiting for us. It was a Dutch ship, the "New Amsterdam," but it was anything but NEW!! It was an old, rusty, dilapidated tub that must have been used by the Vikings!! The crew, that we could see, were mostly Indian (from India) and a conglomeration of other nationalities. There were no bunks for sleeping—only hammocks! This was a new experience! I had never slept in one of those things before!

However, the space we had was too small, and there was absolutely no way that we could stretch the hammock out tight. I got into mine, and my knees came up around my ears!! There was NO way I was going to sleep in that thing! Some of the other guys had the same problem, so we took our blankets, went up on the open deck, found a corner or a nook somewhere, huddled into it and TRIED to sleep. I don't know what we would have done if it had been raining or storming.

There was one passageway that we used most of the times that went past the galley (kitchen) where we could see the Indian cooks preparing our meals as we passed by. We saw large pans of roasted meat, probably mutton, sitting on the floor to cool. As we watched, we saw the cooks and helpers jumping back and forth over the pans of meat as they worked! THAT didn't do much for our appetites! Most of us refused to eat ANY of THAT meat or much of anything else cooked in that kitchen! Then, we found out that we could get small loaves of bread from the ship's bakery. "Well, here's something we can eat as long as we're on this ship," we thought, UNTIL we discovered that the bread came with meat in it!! It had worms in it!! You can be sure that we were a very hungry bunch of guys when we finally got off that ship! Surely Noah and the animals on the Ark had it better than that!! I just wonder what the crew of that ship ate!! Yeeech!

Ordinarily you could cross the English Channel in four or five hours, but it took us one day and one night. We were in a convoy and zigzagging all over the place in order to evade any submarines that might be in the area. In the afternoon of the second day, August 15th, which was D-Day plus seventy days, we dropped anchor off the coast of France. Soon after that, landing boats came alongside our ship and large rope nets were hung over the railings down the side of the ship. Did this mean what I thought it meant? As much as I wanted to get off that ship, I sure wasn't thrilled about getting off THAT way!! We had no choice, though, and one by one we gingerly climbed over the railing. Boy, it sure looked like a loo-oong way down there!! Those landing boats looked awful small—like canoes!! Could I possibly get down that swinging rope net? How could I ever land in that bobbing, bouncing little thing way down there? One slip or one wrong move and you wound up taking a bath! It was certain death IF you dropped off the rope net at the wrong time and you landed in the water between the landing boat and the ship. It would have meant being crushed to death between the two vessels. Thank the Lord that did not happen!

Soon after, we were standing on the beach of Normandy (Omaha Beach, the Army called it), where just seventy days before, terrible fighting had taken place and many men had died. Offshore, we could see many sunken ships, and around us were many blown up tanks, burned out pillboxes and many concrete fortifications the Nazis had built to keep us out.

After picking up our equipment, which had been transported separately, we hiked for about a mile away from the beach to a large field to wait for our transportation. We were still too close to enemy territory and subject to attack by enemy planes and were strictly forbidden to show a light of <u>any</u> kind…not even cigarettes.

There we sat. Five to six hundred men scattered all over that field. After several hours of waiting and wondering, our transportation still had not arrived, and it was starting to get dark. Just as we were wondering where our officers were, a "bright, smart" second Lieutenant appeared and began issuing orders. "Pitch your tents," he ordered.

With a lot of grumbling and griping, we began to open our packs to get our half of the tent and then find someone who had the matching half. Try doing that in the dark sometime!! Some of the men started pitching their tents wherever they were in the field, which meant that our tents would have been scattered all over the field.

When the Lieutenant saw this he screamed, "No, No, NO!! NOT SCATTERED around all over!! I want them in a straight row from one end of the field to the other end!"

WHAT?? We couldn't believe our ears! Surely we didn't hear him right!! ANY dimwit could figure out how stupid that was. If a German plane flew over, he would have a field day! All he would have to do is start at one end of the row, open with his machine guns and go right down the row. He could wipe us out with one sweep!! Besides, what he ordered was completely contrary to everything we had been taught in basic training. Some of the men tried to tell him that and reason with him.

"But sir, that's NOT what we were taught in basic training."

"I don't care WHAT you were taught," he shouted. "I gave you an order. NOW get with it!!"

With a lot more grumbling, some comments on what they thought of smart aleck second Lieutenants, and some swearing (NOT by me!), we went back to moving and trying to pitch our tents in the dark. Thankfully, we heard the rumble of trucks arriving at that moment. Our transportation had finally come!!

Now it was pitch dark—so dark that we couldn't see to get our equipment together. Most of us just threw all our stuff into our tent half and lugged it onto the truck that way. There was NO way that we could repack our packs. We could hardly see to climb into the trucks.

For over two hours, we bounced over rough roads and through bombed out, deserted villages. When we finally stopped and stiffly climbed down from the trucks, we found ourselves in another large field—some French farmer's pasture! We were ordered to spread out, find a good spot, pitch our "pup tent" and hit the sack!! (A pup tent is a two-man tent. You had one half of the tent and you had to find a man who had the matching half. If you had a buddy who had the matching half and you had made arrangements ahead of time, you were okay). Can you imagine the fun we had trying to do that, well after midnight in the pitch dark? There was absolutely NO WAY any of us were going to pitch a tent without a light of some kind. Besides, we were all too tired to bother. We just found a spot, threw our tent half on the ground, threw one blanket on top of it, plopped down on it, pulled our other blanket over us and tried to sleep. As tired as we were, that wasn't too hard to do. Little did we realize that we were "in" our "home" for the next six weeks!!

V
THE COW PASTURE

As daybreak came and men began to stir and move around, the first thing we wanted to see was what kind of place we had landed in. We were on a slightly sloping hillside, in a good-sized field surrounded by hedgerows. These were narrow strips of bushes and small trees used to divide one field from another. I guess they don't believe in fences there, because I never saw any. It turned out to be a busy day for us. We had to find a suitable spot, pitch our tents and get ourselves situated. Some of the men just pitched their tent on the ground while some dug and scooped out a large level spot and pitched their tent over it. We learned the hard way during the first rain that it was necessary to dig a trench around the tent to keep the water from running into the tent. However, I didn't have that problem. The chaplain had a small trailer used to haul all the chapel and office equipment. Since the trailer wasn't going to be used for six weeks, I took the trailer, with the chaplain's permission, parked it under some large trees at the edge of the field, and my buddy Chalmert and I pitched our tent ON it! We could stand up in the tent, which would have been impossible on the ground, and we were up off the ground, too. WE didn't have to worry about getting washed away!! Some of the guys grumbled about it, but there wasn't anything they could do about it. We had our own cozy little nest in a quiet, beautiful spot. Almost like home!!

For a change, there wasn't a whole lot to do, and since there were no suitable places to march and drill (thank goodness!!), we had a lot of free time. One day, a couple of my buddies and I decided to do some exploring and sightseeing. We roamed around in one of the nearby fields, which really wasn't very smart since we saw signs in German warning that there were land mines in the area! They had posted them to warn their own troops, and now they were warning US!! One wrong step and we could have been blown to bits. Hesitating and debating whether or not we should go any further, we suddenly spied a blown up German tank sitting out in the field. We made one beeline for that tank—throwing all caution aside. While we were climbing all over the tank, one of my buddies looked inside.

"Hey fellas," he called, his face turning green, "l-let's get outta here!"

After looking inside, we heartily agreed with him and beat it away from there as fast as we could. Inside that tank were three dead

Germans. THAT really put a damper on any further exploring on our part!!

When we had been in the "Cow Pasture," as we called it, for three or four weeks, some of us got very hungry for some <u>fresh</u> eggs. We decided to do something about it. After all, we were out in the country and there were farms all around us. There's supposed to be chickens and eggs on a farm, ain't there?? So-oo, one day, four of us borrowed the chaplain's jeep and headed out to find some eggs. We drove up a long lane to the first farmhouse we saw, and as we climbed out of the jeep, there stood an elderly farmer and his wife in their yard, watching us with puzzled looks on their faces. They couldn't speak English and we couldn't speak French. None of us knew the French word for "egg," and it had not entered our minds to look it up in our French-English dictionary BEFORE leaving camp!! Of course, we didn't bring it with us either. Really smart, huh? How in the world were we gonna ask these people for eggs? One of the guys took off his helmet and acted like he was putting something into it while one of the other guys squatted down, flapped his hands and cackled like a chicken.

The woman's face lit up and she said, "Oh- Oui, oui" (yes, yes), and grabbing my helmet, she disappeared. Within a few minutes, she reappeared and handed my buddy my helmet. It was all we could do to keep from bursting out laughing.

"Merci" (thank you), we managed to stammer (we knew that much French), as we climbed into the jeep and took off. As soon as we were out of their sight we practically exploded with laughter—our driver could hardly drive! As disappointed as we were, we couldn't help but laugh at the idea of trying to make scrambled eggs out of GREEN APPLES!!!!

The only real problem we had there in the "Cow Pasture" besides mud, were the bees. Not just ordinary bees, these were regular monsters!! They were the biggest bees I ever saw—some almost an inch long, although it seemed like some of them were a foot long!! We did not, as yet, have a mess hall, so we had to sit outside wherever we could find a spot and eat our meals. The bees crawled all over our food, got stuck in our marmalade and drowned in our coffee. They either drowned or the coffee, which we called "battery acid," killed them!! We had to look carefully at every bite just before putting it in our mouth because bees would land on it on the way from your dish to your mouth. Several of the guys got stung on their tongues and had to be hospitalized. Those monsters packed a wallop. I KNOW! One Sunday afternoon, I was lying in my tent relaxing before the evening chapel service. I didn't know that one of these critters had parked on my forehead. I raised my arm to my head putting it right on the bee, and he let me have it! In no time my whole forehead was swollen and my eyes were almost swollen shut. Needless to say, I didn't go to the service that evening, but I can guarantee THAT monster never stung anyone else!!

As if the mud and bees weren't enough to contend with, there was the problem of keeping clean—or should I say, getting clean. For the first three weeks, there was no shower or bath facilities, which some of the guys didn't mind. I guess they figured that if they stank bad enough, the bees would leave them alone (to say nothing about the guys around them!!) Finally, after a lot of complaints and griping, a temporary shower was set up at the backside of the "Cow Pasture." Of course, there was no hot water and it only had space for six men at a time. So, when you finally got in, you had to use just enough water to rinse off and then get out as quickly as possible. There were NO dressing rooms at all. You undressed out in the open, placed your clothes and your towel on benches that were set up on three sides of the shower, took your shower when you could get in and then came out, dried off and dressed very quickly!! Since there wasn't anyone else around, we thought we were okay. However, there was a small dirt road that ran along the back edge of the pasture right past and within twenty-five feet of the shower!! One day, as about twenty-five or thirty of us were waiting to get into the shower or were drying off, all completely undressed or in various stages of undress, a group of about eight or nine young women came merrily strolling down that road right past our shower!! Since this was an open field with no trees or bushes to run behind for cover, we grabbed towels or some piece of clothing to cover and shield ourselves from a bunch of giggling, squealing women! You can be sure that THAT was the last shower that a lot of us took in THAT place!! Although they were impossible to get in to, many of us took our "baths" from our helmets—at least until we got somewhere where we could take a shower in privacy!!

Of course, there were no laundromats, no washing machines or tubs to wash clothes in, so having clean clothes was a problem. Loafing around in a cow pasture (although WE never saw any cows there!) all day doesn't do much for keeping clean. One of my buddies found a five-gallon can, and with water from the creek that flowed through one end of the pasture and soap from who knows where, he produced hot, soapy water over a campfire and did his laundry. He shared his "washing machine" with some of his other buddies so THEY had clean clothes—even if they were wrinkled! Most of us gave up trying to do our laundry in our helmets, except for small items such as socks and underwear, since it was so hard to get hot water or soap. None of us wanted to heat our water in our helmets and we just couldn't find anything else. I never did find out where my buddy found that five-gallon can!!

We sure weren't the cleanest or neatest bunch of characters when we finally left the "Cow Pasture," but I'm sure we were the smelliest!!

It was with no regrets that we packed up and left the "Cow Pasture." After six weeks of living in those two-man tents, being out in the open continually and having to use our helmets to shave, bathe and do our laundry, all in cold water, we were definitely ready for a change. That old "Cow Pasture" was one place we would just as soon forget, but I'll have to admit that there were SOME pleasant

moments—in spite of the monster bees and the lack of privacy!!

Our Hospital - Leominster, England 1944

England, 1944

1944 – 45 76th General Hospital
Liege, Belgium

Liege, Belgium ~ 1945
After My Hair Grew Back Out!

Our Hospital - December 1944

December 1944

Old Chapel
Protestant Chaplain's Office
(Rear) – Catholic Chaplain's Office

Our Chaplain

My Boss! - 1944

Our New Chapel   Inside the Chapel

View From Front Door

Altar In Old Chapel

We Actually Had A
Wedding In This Chapel!

Remagen Bridge where U.S. troops first entered
Germany.

St. Vith, Belgium 1945

St. Vith, or what's left of it.

SGT. Harold Gale,
our Mess Sergeant

Midnight Snack in Surgery, with my Buddy ~ CPL. Ernest
Voellings, Nurse LT. Moore, and Doctor Capt. Meyer. We were
having <u>fresh</u> fried eggs!

Our "Adopted" Children

Marcel Bawin

Andrea Peters

Their Fathers were executed by the Nazis because of their
involvement in the Underground movement.

Andrea and her sister Leonce

Marcel – 1st Communion

Andrea, Marcel, Leonce, and me, in front of our chapel. 1945

That's me. The week following January 8, 1945 when our hospital was hit by a "Buzz" bomb.

The monument to the 25 men lost on January 8, 1945

Erected at the main entrance of our hospital

Malmedy, Belgium – 1945
At this spot, during the
Battle of the Bulge,
American soldiers were
herded into this field and
then machine-gunned to
death by Nazi S.S. troops.
The huge concrete cross and
the engraved stones on each
side were erected by the
Belgian people.

Malmedy, Belgium - 1945

Bernhard Klostermeyer and me
just before I left Liege for the last
time.

ZUSTERS NORBERTIENEN VAN DUFFEL
BETHANIENHUIS
Sint-Antonius-Brecht

Antwerp, Belgium
Our last stop in Belgium. This Belgian hospital, we didn't operate
here as a hospital, we just stayed there.

Aunt Elsa and Uncle Fritz Roswitha and
Brunhilde Nagel.
The first ones I saw on my way to see Grandma.
July, 1945

My Grandma, Christine Feucht and me.
The last time I had seen her was in 1934 when I
was 9. One of my Aunts took this picture. I think
she was concentrating on me! July, 1945

VI
GOODBYE FRANCE, HELLO BELGIUM

As usual, when we left the "Cow Pasture" we had no idea where we were going. Were we surprised when we arrived in Paris, France! What a change!! We were living in what had been a small hotel at one time. We actually had a SOLID roof over our heads!! BUT our hopes for a good time of sightseeing in Paris were dashed when we were informed upon our arrival that there would be NO passes! All I saw of Paris was what I saw out of the back of a truck. I did see a few landmarks as I went on various errands for the chaplain, (being the chaplain's assistant had its advantages!)—but only from a distance. Since we couldn't get passes to get out and really see the city, and as we learned shortly after arriving, we would not be stationed in Paris, this was only another stopping point on the way. We were anxious to move on. That came after we had been there one week! Would we ever settle down again, somewhere??

It was while we were in Paris that I got a letter from home informing me that I had a new little brother!! Talk about being shocked and surprised!! I ran around telling everybody, "Hey, I've got a new little brother!! How about that?" I didn't know then that he would be almost a year and a half old before I would ever see him.

One evening, a few days before we left Paris, several of us were sitting around in what had been the kitchen, writing letters and talking. Suddenly, the conversation turned to religion and whether there is life after death. This gave me a great opening, and I was able to talk to them about the Lord.

After we had talked for some time, as they were interested and receptive, one of the men, Ben, said, "Karl, I wish I had what you've got."

"You can, Ben," I answered, eager to lead him to the Lord. Ben was quite a bit older than me, and since none of us knew what lay ahead of us, I wanted very much to help these guys get ready for whatever came.

"Not now," Ben answered. "I'm just not ready yet. I'll talk to you some more one of these days and then maybe I will."

"Okay Ben," I said with a heavy heart. "Any time you are ready." Sadly, that day never came. A few days later we were on our way out of Paris.

It was a cold, gray day when we arrived in Liege (Lee-edge), Belgium. We had mixed feelings when we saw rows of tents and realized that THIS was our next hospital and home. EVERYTHING was tents!! So much for our hopes of living in a solid building! We were given mattress covers and straw to stuff into them. These were then placed on a folding Army cot—our beds for the next eight and a half months!!

Liege, an industrial city, is one of the largest cities in Belgium and lies in a large valley. Our hospital was located on top of a hill on one side of the city, and we could look across a part of the city and see the hills on the other side of the valley, a distance of approximately four miles. We were also thirteen miles from the German border and fifteen miles from the city of Aachen, Germany. When we arrived in Liege, American troops were just approaching Aachen; they had not yet captured the city. We could hear the big guns booming, and at night the sky to the east of us was red from the fires of burning buildings. It was an eerie feeling knowing that we were that close to the actual fighting.

The first few weeks were really busy—getting the hospital equipment and beds set up, and in my case, getting the chapel and the chaplain's office set up. Since the Catholic chaplain didn't have an assistant, I served as his assistant also, except for the Catholic masses. A month later he was given his own assistant, for which I was very,

very thankful as he was not an easy man to work for. I was supposed to drive the chaplain's jeep taking him wherever he needed to go, but since I had just started learning to drive when I entered the Army and had no driver's license, a regular driver was assigned to the chaplain. I didn't mind too much, for as a passenger I could see more of the scenery!!

Our chow was fair for Army chow considering that we were in another country and all our food had to be transported. We heard that people back in the States were complaining because they couldn't buy good cuts of meat anymore. They were told that most of the "good" meat was being sent to "boys" overseas! HA!! We had beef stew (it was supposed to be beef!) a number of times. The gravy and vegetables were fine and edible, but eating the big chunks of beef in it was utterly impossible. You couldn't even stick a fork into it, much less CHEW it!! One guy took a couple pieces of the meat one time and put it down on the floor for one of the many skinny, scrawny dogs that always roamed around in our mess tent looking for handouts and scraps. This particular dog was really skinny and hungry looking. He sniffed at the meat, nudged it with his nose and WALKED AWAY!!

"LOOK AT THAT," the guy that put the meat down yelled, drawing the attention of everyone in the mess tent. "THE DOG WON'T EVEN EAT IT AND THEY EXPECT US TO EAT IT!!"

What was even sadder, to me anyway, was that all the scraps and stuff that we threw into the garbage can on our way out of the mess hall was immediately dug out by Belgian civilians and taken home for the "dinner" that night. The "good" meat we were supposed to be getting went to the officers. It sure didn't come to us!!

A half-mile from our hospital was the Prisoner of War stockade where approximately 300 German prisoners were living. Every morning they were marched, under guard, to the hospital where they went to their various assigned duties. They were responsible for the care of the grounds, some worked in the wards cleaning up and others did any construction work that was needed. One prisoner was assigned to the chapel and it was my job to keep him busy!! Since I spoke German, I had no problem telling him what to do. Bernhardt was a blonde eighteen-year old, the same age as I was. For the first few weeks he was <u>very</u> military and formal in spite of the fact that I tried in every way I could think of to be friendly with him. I felt that if we were going to be together all day, six days a week, we could at least be friendly. I saw him as a lonely, young boy away from his home and family, just like me. I didn't see him as an enemy or a monster waiting to pounce on me at any moment. After all, HIS fighting days were over. He did everything he was told to do and did it well. He was a good worker, but he just wasn't friendly. It was as if a wall existed between us. That wall was his military training and the things he had been taught about the horrible, monster Americans. It was as if he expected me to suddenly raise up a gun and shoot him! I received a package from home, which contained some of my Mom's homemade cookies and other good things. When I offered him some, he refused; only after I kept insisting did he finally take some. I don't know if he thought they were poisoned until he saw me eat some and then decided they must be okay. I think the big thing was that he couldn't believe that he was being treated kindly. He never spoke without calling me "Sir," and I was only a Corporal! After about two weeks of his "military" nonsense, I came to the office on Friday morning praying that the Lord would help me say or do something that day that would break down the "wall" that stood between us.

Shortly after, Bernhardt came in with a snappy, "Good morning, Sir," (in German of course because he spoke no English).

He stood at attention waiting for me to give him his work for the day. After I did so, he informed me that he would not be there the next day as Saturday was his day off. Each prisoner was given one day off each week to take care of his own needs such as cleaning his tent, doing his laundry, helping maintain the stockade and relaxing. Another prisoner was assigned to fill in for him on Saturdays. That afternoon when it was time for him to report to the assembly area to march back to the stockade, he came into the office and waited at attention for me to dismiss him. He never left until I dismissed him. By this time, in answer to my prayer, God had given me an idea. I knew that he had to go across the path into the back of the chapel where he had hung his jacket and cap that morning.

"Go get your jacket and cap," I told him, "and I will be right over."

After putting his jacket on, he stood up with cap in hand, waiting for me to tell him that he could go. Instead, I stepped up to him, put my left hand on his shoulder, took his right hand in mine and said, "You won't be here tomorrow, right?"

As long as I live, I will NEVER forget the look of complete surprise on his face when I put my hand on his shoulder. It was some time before he was able to speak to answer my question.

"J--Ja," he stammered, with tears in his eyes.

"Then have a good day tomorrow, Bernhardt, and I'll see you Sunday morning," I said as he suddenly squeezed my hand.

He stood there for a short time firmly gripping my hand, unable to speak. Then, letting go of my hand, he turned, went through the chapel and when he got to the rear door, he opened it, turned and gave me a big sunny smile, waved and left. The Lord had answered my prayer!! I KNEW the wall was gone!! When Bernhardt came into the office Sunday morning, it was as if a completely different person came in. The "military" was gone and so were the "sirs"!!! From that day on, we worked, laughed and joked together, and I began to talk to him about the Lord. What a joy it was for me, when one morning he knelt in my tent, tears streaming down his cheeks and accepted Jesus as his Savior. After he had wept and prayed for some time, I asked him, "Bernhardt, what happened?"

Looking up at me through his tears, his face glowing with a light that had not been there before, he answered, "Jesus came into my heart!"

I was finally beginning to understand WHY I was there! This ONE German boy coming to Jesus was worth all my unanswered prayers, although they weren't really "un-answered." God just answered them in His own way!! And, He wasn't through yet!!

Bernhardt was not the only German prisoner I was to be involved with. One day, the chaplain informed me that according to the Articles of War, an agreement between all Nations, he was responsible to see that the prisoners had church services if they wanted them.

"I can't do it," he said. "I don't speak German. Do you think you can do it?" He knew that I spoke German.

"Oh no—NO way," I replied. "I don't speak German well enough to do THAT!"

"Do you know of anybody that could?" he asked. "There's a couple of men here in our outfit who were born in Germany. Would you recommend any of them?"

"Definitely NOT! They are not Christians, and there is NO way they could get up and preach to anybody! I know those men, and they are very ungodly men."

"Well, what are we going to do?" he asked, hoping that I would say that I would do it. He said, "I suppose I could go down to the main prisoner stockade in Luxembourg and see if I can find a prisoner who was a minister before the war."

"Yes sir, that might work," I agreed, knowing that wasn't what he wanted to hear.

As it turned out, the chaplain made <u>two</u> trips to Luxembourg with NO success. It seemed as if every outfit in Europe was looking for men who had been ministers. How the Lord was working to accomplish His purposes! I'm glad that He knew what He was doing!! Finally, in desperation the chaplain, tired of fooling around with his balky, thickheaded assistant, came to me.

"Karl, I've got to do something. I don't <u>want</u> to pull rank on you, but if I have to, okay. I'm going to <u>order</u> you to conduct the services for the prisoners. I'll help you all I can. I'll give you some of my sermon notes to use if that will help."

"Okay sir, I'll give it a try," I answered reluctantly and with a lot of doubt.

I still couldn't see the great opportunity the Lord was giving me, but I think the chaplain did, and the Lord was using him to help me.

"Great!" he said with a big smile and a sigh of relief. "I'm sure with the Lord's help, you'll do just fine."

Even then, I didn't feel as sure and confident as he did! "What am I getting into?" I wondered.

I spent the next week, with the help of every German-English dictionary I could get my hands on, translating one of the chaplain's sermons into German. I got it all except for a few words here and there, which I simply skipped over when I gave the sermon! Have you ever heard a sermon with a lot of "holes" in it? Is that what you would call a "holy" sermon??

That first Sunday and first sermon was a real experience for me. When the chaplain and I entered the stockade, all the prisoners who wanted to attend the service, about sixty or seventy men, were all standing in formation! As we approached, they immediately snapped to attention and remained so until they were allowed to break ranks and go into the tent where the service was to be held. I didn't know any German hymns or church songs, so after explaining this to them, I told them to sing three or four hymns that they all knew. They sang several songs that I assumed were hymns—they sounded like hymns!! I then read several scriptures from my German Bible and then read (or stumbled) through my sermon. After a brief prayer, I dismissed them. THAT was the beginning of my "ministry," which was to continue every Sunday evening for almost a year, AND I finally began to realize—THAT was why God had me there!!

As soon as we returned to the office, the chaplain turned to me. "Karl, I won't go with you anymore. You are on your own from now on. The presence of an officer—he was a Captain—just causes too much tension and hinders you. Those prisoners have so much Army and "military discipline" drilled into them that they can't just relax when an officer is present. I feel that my being there is more of a hindrance than a help."

"Yes sir," I agreed. "I felt that too, and chaplain, if you don't mind, I'd just as soon get my own sermons from now on instead of having to translate your sermons."

With a big smile on his face, the chaplain looked at me. "Good!!" he said. "I was hoping you would do that! Since you are planning to go into the ministry after you get out of the Army, this will be good training and experience for you. I'll help you all I can and I'll certainly be praying for you. Just let me know if you need me."

The next Sunday and from then on, the services were much more relaxed. My German actually began to improve so that there weren't any more blank spaces in my sermons, and above all, I was accepted by the prisoners. I will NEVER forget the look on their faces that second Sunday when I delivered my sermon. "I don't hate YOU," I told them. "I hate what you have stood for: Nazi-ism. Jesus loves you and I do too."

Many of them had never heard anything like that before. The Nazis didn't teach things like that! From then on, I was their friend as far as they were concerned, but believe me, I got plenty of remarks and criticism from some of our own guys. After all, these Germans were the enemy; I was supposed to hate them and have nothing to do with them, but I couldn't and didn't see it that way. Didn't Jesus Himself tell us that we should "love our enemies"??

The prisoners were very open and hungry for the Word of God. Many Sundays I was there two hours and more AFTER the service was over with a group of the prisoners around me asking questions about Jesus and the Bible. I was really touched by their hunger for God's Word. Most of the younger prisoners had never heard these things before. They had no idea that God loved them and that Jesus died for them. The prisoners had no Bibles and they began begging for Bibles. WHERE was I going to get German Bibles?? I had had a hard time getting one for myself!! However, with the chaplain's help and the help of a chaplain friend of his, I managed to come up with a dozen Bibles within two weeks. Twelve Bibles for almost a hundred men!! I saw something I had never seen before and never thought I would ever see—men almost coming to blows, fighting over a Bible!! I finally set up a system where one man had a Bible for one week. At the end of his week, he passed it on to another man for the next week. During the week that a man had a Bible, I encouraged him to share it with the others by reading to them. Because the prisoners were very cooperative, everything worked out fine. They really treasured those Bibles!

Every Sunday evening after checking in at the stockade office, I went into the stockade to the "chapel" for our service. I never had a guard with me, and of course I never carried a weapon. Was I nervous or afraid? NO!! Because I knew that the Lord was with me. After all, wasn't He the One who got me into this situation? I also knew that IF any prisoner had tried in ANY way to harm me, he would have had ten or twenty other prisoners on him in a flash!! Even prisoners who never attended the services! I had their trust; there wasn't anything within their power that they wouldn't do for me. They found out that we weren't going to torture, starve or kill them as they had been taught by their Nazi teachers. We Americans were not the horrible monsters the Nazis said we were. Many prisoners, right after they were captured, cried openly when they were given their first full, hot meal and clean warm clothing. They just couldn't believe it!! THAT wasn't what they had been told and taught!! Some of them even wished that they could contact some of their friends and relatives who were still fighting in the German Army and tell them to surrender!!

By this time, I knew why the Lord hadn't answered my prayers the way I THOUGHT He should. I was exactly where HE wanted me and THAT was the important thing.

VII
V-1'S, V-2: "BUZZ BOMBS"

Shortly after arriving in Liege, I was outside one sunny afternoon between the office tent and the chapel tent adjusting the tent ropes, when I heard a strange sound coming from the East out of Germany. It sounded something like a plane, but I knew that it was not a plane. As I looked in the direction from where the sound was coming, I saw a dark speck high in the sky growing larger and larger as it approached. When it passed directly over our hospital, I realized that I was looking at a German V-1 bomb, or "buzz bomb," as they came to be called. It passed over the city of Liege on its way to England. This was the first of many that we were going to see. We learned later that they were launched in Germany from a catapult after it was determined where they wanted them to land. They would estimate the distance from the point of launching to the city where it was to land, determine the amount of fuel needed to get it there and then aim and launch it.

There were three types of V-1 bombs. The first, and most common, was when the bomb was over its target and it ran out of fuel, the motor shut off, the nose of the bomb tipped downward and the bomb plunged to hit its target. The second type was when the bomb slowed down just enough to cause the nose of the bomb to tip downward and then plunge to the earth, its motor running until it hit the target. The third type was when the bomb approached within two or three miles of the target, it ran out of fuel, the motor shut off and the bomb glided the rest of the way until it hit the target. You never heard it coming. Little did we realize as we watched these bombs passing over us that we would soon experience all three types of this 2,000 pound horror. The explosion upon impact was terrific and the shock waves could be felt four and five miles away.

THE V-1 "BUZZ BOMB"

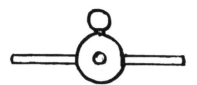

HEAD-ON VIEW

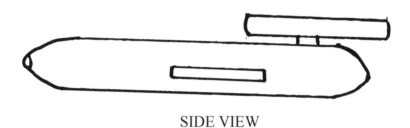

SIDE VIEW

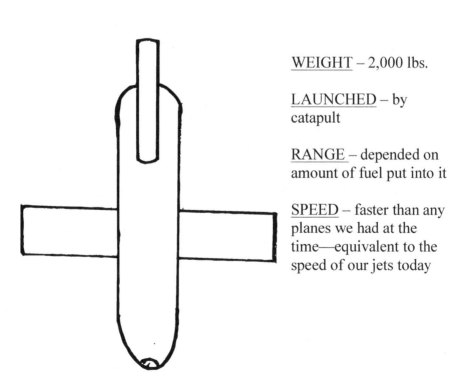

WEIGHT – 2,000 lbs.

LAUNCHED – by catapult

RANGE – depended on amount of fuel put into it

SPEED – faster than any planes we had at the time—equivalent to the speed of our jets today

It wasn't long after this that not ALL of the bombs were going over to England. Some of them began to fall in the city of Liege. Gradually, more and more of them fell into the city and around our hospital and fewer of them went on to England. It seemed as if Liege was becoming the main target. It got so that whenever we heard one coming, we would run outside, if possible, to see if it was coming over the hospital, hoping that it wouldn't come down on us!! It eventually got to the point where one or two guys would go out, see where the bomb was heading, then call back into the rest of us. He might say, "On track one or two, three or four to the right or to the left." Track one was the only one we were concerned about because that meant it was coming right over us!! When we heard "track one" we ALL scrambled out at once—fast!!

On clear days, we could always see the bomb moving along. They looked like small planes with short, stubby wings. At night, we could see a tail of flame coming from the exhaust on the top rear of the bomb as it moved through the sky. We could ALWAYS hear them, even on cloudy days, unless it was a type three bomb (see illustration). On very rare occasions, a bomb would malfunction. One afternoon, a bomb came directly over the hospital and suddenly started going around in circles over us. There we stood, watching that crazy thing, unable to do anything about it. Was it going to stop and come down?? WHAT was it going to do??? After circling in big circles seven or eight times, it finally veered off and landed in a field a short distance from us!! Wheeewww!! THAT was too close for comfort!! It's a wonder any of us had any fingernails left after that!!

About nine o'clock one evening, as I sat on my cot in my tent, I heard a plane flying over us, but as I listened it dawned on me that he was NOT flying over—he was circling around over us!! I knew it was not one of our planes. This one had the higher pitched whine of a German plane. Without thinking, I ran outside to see what was going on. Apparently, as he was flying over at a low altitude, one of our guards, thinking he would be a "big hero," got trigger happy and fired at the plane. IF he had hit the plane, it would have been an absolute miracle. Seeing this, the pilot turned and began circling over the hospital. He obviously was confused. Although it was dark, he probably could see the huge white circles with big red crosses painted on the top of every tent, indicating that this was a hospital. The Germans respected the Red Cross and hospitals and did not fire on them. BUT—neither did hospitals fire on the Germans!! Someone had fired at him! I saw him suddenly swoop down, heard his machine guns as he opened fire and saw the tracers streaming down toward the ground. One sweep and he was gone! The next morning we heard that he had hit the nurses' quarters. Fortunately, the nurses living in the tents he hit were all on duty at that time. One of the nurses had received a package from home that day and had invited some of her friends to her tent for cookies and coffee shortly before going on duty. When they had finished, they put all the coffee mugs in a dishpan to be washed later. One of the bullets fired by that pilot ripped through the tent and went through one of the mugs in that dishpan taking the bottom out of it as neatly as if it had been cut out!

Later, the nurse who owned that mug, although somewhat shaken and shocked, commented to her friends, "I ought to make that German buy me a new mug!!"

Although he was the enemy, I had to give that German pilot credit. At least he did not fire into the hospital itself, but at the tents at the very edge. Those tents were not marked with Red Crosses. Of course, that pilot had no way of knowing that those tents were the nurses' quarters and also the officers and enlisted men's quarters. As it was, no one was hit or killed.

Meanwhile, the "buzz bombs" kept coming over in even greater numbers. One night between 10 P.M. and 6 A.M., some of the men on night duty counted over sixty bombs that passed over our hospital!! No wonder many of us were becoming nervous wrecks! In fact, several officers and enlisted men had to be sent back to hospitals in England because their nerves snapped, but we NEVER lost a nurse!! Only one nurse had to be sent back to another hospital because she had slipped on an icy walk and fractured her leg. It was really amazing how well those ladies held up during this time—and during the horror that was yet to come. They sure were an encouragement and inspiration to a lot of younger guys!

VIII
DARK DAYS

December 16, 1944, a cold snowy, gloomy day brought with it even more gloom. Early in the morning, just before daybreak, the German Army launched a massive, surprise attack, which became known as the "Battle of the Bulge." Finding a weak spot in our lines, they broke through and were soon advancing rapidly into Belgium, headed in our direction, and it seemed as if they were not going to be stopped! We were glued to every radio we could find, listening to every news report and looking at our maps to see how close they were getting to us. German soldiers, dressed in American uniforms taken off dead American G.I.s, began filtering through our lines to do as much damage as they could. Most of them could speak English. As a result, a new password was issued each day, and before we could go out on a pass or ANYWHERE, we had to get the password for the day. If you got stopped, and you often were, you'd better know the current password or you were in a heap of trouble. The passwords were always words that were hard for Germans to say even if they spoke very good English. For example, one day when the chaplain and I were out on some business, the password for that day was "thunder weather." There is NO German anywhere who can say that unless he has really mastered the English language. The closest they can come to saying that is "dunder vetter." Very few Germans can say the "th," and in German the "W" is said like a "V." In this way, many of the imposters were caught. My dad, born in Germany, lived in America for almost sixty years and he never did learn to correctly pronounce many English words! That old German accent just kept coming through!!

After three or four days of listening to the radio and marking our maps, we were really on edge. The Germans were getting uncomfortably close. Then, one night we heard all kinds of tanks, armored vehicles and big guns rumbling past on the main highway a half-mile from the hospital, all headed for the front lines. The thing was, WE didn't know WHERE those front lines were!! I found out the next morning. One of my buddies operated the hospital switchboard handling all incoming and outgoing messages. He told me that German paratroopers had landed FOUR miles from our hospital during the night and THAT is where all that armored equipment we heard was going!! Another message had also come in to our commanding officer, Colonel Fancher, placing our hospital "on alert" which meant that we were to be ready to leave at a moment's notice. That next morning, we were all called out into formation and were given instructions on what to do IF orders came for us to leave. We would be divided into three groups. The first group would load all the patients that could be moved into every available vehicle (ambulances, trucks and jeeps), and leave as quickly as possible. The second group would be designated to remain behind to care for the patients that could not be moved. All the others would be in the third group. They were to dress as warmly as possible, stuff their pockets with extra socks and underclothes, take any food, candy bars, etc., they could manage and take off, heading away from the advancing German Army. Since I spoke and understood German, there was NO doubt in MY mind which group I would be in. I would be in group two—remaining behind. Thankfully, that order to leave never came. After five or six days of fierce fighting, the German advance was stopped, much to our relief, and they were gradually driven back to Germany. NOW, we were able to breathe easier and think about Christmas just a few days away.

Satisfied that the chapel was ready for the Christmas Eve service the next day, Sunday, I turned off the lights, closed the chapel and headed for my tent—and bed. Bernhardt and I had worked hard all day getting the chapel ready, and I was tired and ready to plop into my cot. I figured that if I had the chapel ready the night before, I could sleep longer in the morning. HA! THAT'S what I thought! Herr Hitler had other ideas!

Early Sunday morning, I awoke suddenly out of a sound sleep, and seeing that it was still dark, I tried to go back to sleep. Besides, it was COLD because the fire in the stove had gone out. Brrrr!! Who wants to crawl out of a nice warm bed when it's freezing when they don't have to??

As I snuggled further down under the covers, a little voice inside stirred. "Get up now," it said.

There in the darkness and with eleven other men snoring around me, I actually argued with that little voice inside me. "I don't want to get up now. The chapel is all ready, and I can sleep for a couple more hours."

"Get up, NOW," the voice said again more urgently.

"I DON'T WANT to get up now," I insisted as I turned on my side to go back to sleep. No matter how hard I tried, flopping from one side to the other, I could NOT go back to sleep.

Then, the voice came again more emphatic and insistent than before. "GET UP NOW!!"

Throwing the covers off me, I quickly got out of bed, dressed as fast as I could because of the cold, made my bed and headed for the office. Since it was still very early, I knew the chaplain would not be there for some time, so I had the office all to myself. After spending some time in prayer and asking the Lord to protect me through the day, I began to read my Bible. Suddenly I heard it!! The unmistakable sound of a "buzz bomb!" I jumped up, ran out the door and looked in the direction of the sound. Yep, there it was! It was still dark enough so that I could see the flame from its exhaust as it moved along. It was coming directly over the hospital!! I watched it as it moved along until it was right over the heart of the hospital. Suddenly, the nose tipped downward and that bomb started coming down—straight at me! I dropped to the ground, remembering to keep my chest off the ground so that the concussion from the explosion would not collapse my lungs and kill me. I turned and looked up at that horrid thing and this is what I saw... ⎯⦵⎯ ...coming right at me.

"This is it," I thought. "I'm going to be with Jesus in a few seconds." I fully expected to be blown to bits in the next few seconds. There was no way that I could run fast enough or get far enough away to avoid being killed. "I wonder how Mom and Dad will take it when they get the news?" I thought.

All these thoughts went through my mind in the few seconds I was there on the ground watching that bomb plunging toward me. What happened next HAD to be the hand of God. When that 2,000 pound bomb was approximately 300 feet above me, the nose suddenly raised up, the bomb leveled out and soared over me to the edge of our living quarters and landed in the road that ran between our quarters and the hospital, blasting a hole in the road big enough to hold a full-sized, two-story house with room to spare!! Fortunately, no one was killed and there were no serious injuries—just a lot of tent damage, a few cuts and bruises and a bunch of shook up G.I.s—of which I was the main one!! Shook up—but VERY thankful!!

I immediately jumped up, checked the office which was total mess and then ran through the chapel which was an even greater mess! All our hard work and preparations the day before were for nothing!! Benches were thrown every which way as if they had been thrown into the tent. The platform and altar were wrecked and the tent itself was halfway blown in and was full of holes. That pretty well took care of our Christmas service that day. However, the chaplain was scheduled to conduct services that afternoon for another outfit in our area, which did not have a chaplain. That meant work for me, as I was responsible for the folding organ, which I played, the case of hymnals and the altar set-up for the service. When we returned from the service later that afternoon, I was in the process of unloading the equipment from the jeep when one of the men who slept in the same tent I did was passing by.

As soon as he saw me he yelled out to me. "Hey Karl! You're sure lucky you didn't sleep this morning as long as you usually do!"

"Why?" I asked, knowing that I had actually planned to sleep in longer than usual that morning.

"Oh, you'll find out when you go down to your tent," he answered and went on his way.

Now, I was curious; I could hardly wait to get to my tent, but I wasn't able to make it until late that evening. When I finally stepped into my tent and looked to the other end where my cot was, I KNEW then that it was the Lord that woke me up that morning and told me to "get up." With tears in my eyes, I stood there and said out loud, "Thank you, Jesus."

Directly above my bed was a large hole about the size of a basketball where a large chunk of that bomb had ripped through and landed on my bed where my head would have been had I been in it!! At the foot of my bed was another hole in the side of the tent where another piece of that bomb had ripped through piercing halfway through my gas mask that was hanging there. I had to get a new gas mask. One thing for SURE, after that day, IF I am awakened early and told to get up, I won't lie there and argue and try to go back to sleep!! After all, when you know the Lord is watching over you AND He proves it by snatching you out of the jaws of death TWO times in one day—well, it's time to sit up and take notice and start believing His WORD and His promises. I sure don't think He brought me over here and gave me this ministry with the prisoners to just let me be killed. He can even control the bombs!!

It was during this time that we had another example of all the "good" meat we were supposed to be getting. Because of the attack by Germans, our supply lines were cut, making it impossible to get any supplies through to us. As a result, the only meat we had for three weeks was canned SPAM! By the end of those three weeks, most of us never wanted to SEE Spam again, much less EAT it!!

IX
PLEASE, HERR HITLER...STOP!!

Damage from Herr Hitler's "Christmas present" was nearly cleaned up and repaired when   January 8, 1945, dawned cold and dreary with three inches of snow on the ground. Again, I woke up earlier than I needed to, and although I felt no urging to get up right then, though now I do believe the Lord woke me up, I got up anyway. It was just after 7A.M. when I arrived at the office and spent some time in prayer and Bible reading. Since my Belgian laundry lady was coming later that morning to pick up my laundry, I proceeded to sort and make a list of all the clothes that I was sending out. We had to make a list of each and every piece, because a lot of the time there would be items missing when it came back. At least, with a list we knew what was stolen!! Around 8 A.M. I suddenly heard a strange sound---Brrrrp---Brrrrp---as if someone was trying to start a motor. The only motor near the chapel was the generator just outside the theater (see map), which furnished power for the projector.

"Yeah, that's it," I thought. "But wait, WHO would be starting THAT at this time of the morning?? They only use that at night when they have movies!!" As I turned to resume sorting my laundry, a thought hit me like a flash. "Hey, IF that's not a motor, then it must be a BOMB—and if it sounds like THAT, it must be coming down around here!!"

Immediately, I dropped to the floor in the middle of all my dirty laundry. My knees no sooner hit the floor, when a terrific loud explosion blasted everything around me. The wooden door built into the entrance of the tent was blown wide open, the light bulb in the light was completely blown away, everything on the chaplain's desk and mine was blown off AND all the keys, reeds and parts of the Catholic chaplain's folding organ, which I was attempting to repair and which I had so very carefully laid out so I'd be sure to get them put back in the proper order, were blown all over the office!! Would I EVER find all those pieces and get that organ put back together again so it could be played???

As soon as the noise of the explosion died away, I jumped to my feet and headed for the door. I got TO the door, but I COULD NOT GO THROUGH THAT DOOR!!! It was as if someone was standing in that doorway, blocking it and keeping me from going out!! The moment I stopped, I heard something hit the ground just outside the door. Then I realized that there was a lot of debris falling around, and since I didn't have my helmet on, it just wasn't the smartest thing to go out just then! I squatted down, covered my head with my arms and waited until I no longer heard anything falling outside. Jumping up, I ran through the door—unhindered—and ran into the chapel to check on damage and to make sure that there was no danger of fire from the stove. The place was a total mess, worse than before. When everything was secure, I ran to the area where the bomb hit, unprepared for what I saw there.

The bomb was a type three bomb. It had shut off some distance from the hospital and had glided until it hit. For some reason, the motor had sputtered twice, which was very unusual—they rarely ever did that once the motor shut off. I think the Lord had something to do with that because it was the sound I had heard and it gave me time to react. It might have been worse for me if I had been standing up.

The shifts had changed at 7A.M. and many of the night shifts were already in bed. There were two tents in which most of the night shift slept, and that bomb landed right between those two tents. Those men never knew what hit them. ONE man living in one of those tents escaped ONLY because he was in the restroom at that moment! When he realized what a close call he had, he was unable to stand up for some time. He was so shocked his legs just wouldn't hold him up!! All told, twenty-five men died that morning—one of them was Ben, the man who told me in Paris that he "wished he could have what I had" and that he "would talk to me about it again another day." Regretfully, I never had a chance to talk to him again—THAT day never came. I hope and pray that he wasn't too late. Two other boys, the only ones from my hometown of Dayton, Ohio, also died that day. All they ever found of the one boy was his head. Many others were injured.

As I got close to where the bomb had hit, I was shocked at what I saw—the horror of war. All the trees around the area that still had branches left on them had shreds of clothing, blankets and tent canvas hanging from them. Our company office, Post Office and our supply tent were completely gone. When I saw that, I KNEW that again the Lord had awakened me early. IF I had gone to the office at my usual time, I would have been walking right past our company office and Post Office at the exact moment the bomb hit!!! THAT was the LORD—NOT luck!!

When I entered the area looking to see where I could help, I saw a man to my left, sitting in the mud and snow, rocking back and forth and crying, "Oh God, Oh God---Oh Mother, Oh Mother." He died shortly after that.

Moving on, I saw a couple of men digging frantically in the mud. One of the men had dug a trench under his cot so that when a bomb was coming, he could dive into it for protection. When the bomb hit, it blasted him, cot and all, into the trench and caused the trench to cave in burying him alive. When I got there, the men digging had just reached him, but it was too late—he was dead.

I wasn't used to this kind of thing, and I was getting pretty shook up. I wanted to get away from there…fast!! I had seen enough of war!

As I turned away to leave, I saw another man at the base of a tree. He looked as if he had been sitting up and had fallen forward on his face. No one was around him, so I ran over to him and just as I got to him, another man arrived at the same time. As we got on each side of him, the man who had just arrived said, "Let's raise him up and lay him on his back."

Taking him by the shoulders, we slowly raised him up. When he was almost in a sitting position, we both took one look and let him fall back down. We had been looking at his intestines. He was split open clear across his mid-section. There was nothing to be done for him.

NOW I REALLY wanted to get away from there. I didn't want to see anymore, so I headed for the office. Just as I reached the road, an ambulance backed up to the edge of the road. I leapt to the back of the ambulance, yanked the doors open and began pulling out the stretchers to be used to carry the wounded and dead to the ambulance and to make room in the ambulance for those that were coming. Just a short time before this, the prisoners had arrived from the stockade for their days work in the hospital. They were immediately ordered to spread out and search the whole area for parts of bodies, needed for identification as some of the men had been blown to pieces. Two men were never found nor any parts of them were ever found.

As I stood there waiting for stretchers with patients to come, wondering what I could do next and hoping I could get away from there real soon, I heard someone speaking behind me. They were speaking in German, so I knew they must be speaking to me.

"Was soll ich mit das tun?" (What should I do with this?)

I turned to see who was speaking to me and saw the youngest prisoner in the stockade, a small, skinny, scared, sixteen-year old boy. In his hand he held someone's arm, an arm from the elbow down— including the whole hand. THAT did it!! I waved both hands at him and said, "Ich weiss nicht!!" (I don't know!!)

I turned away and made a beeline for the office. There I sat at my desk for the rest of the day, staring into space, too shocked and numb to do anything. When the chaplain came in and talked to me, I answered in little, short sentences, hardly aware of what I was saying. For the next week, I was like a robot. Everything I did was mechanical, as if I was in a daze. I couldn't eat or sleep. During the day, I put in my time in the office, and at night, I went to one of the wards where one of my buddies worked the night shift and helped care for the patients. One night while I was on the ward, one of the men who had been badly injured by the bomb suddenly lapsed into a coma. We immediately called the O.D. (officer of the day), who came at once and began working on him. The doctor, the nurse, my buddy and I worked on him for over an hour, but he died as we were doing all we could to save him: another blow to my already shattered nerves. By the end of the week, I was really in bad shape. The chaplain was aware of it too, because he came into the office one morning and the first thing he said was, "Karl, I want you to get out of this office! I don't want to use my rank on you, but I am ordering you to get out of here, and I don't want you to come back in here anymore today. Go some place, do something—ANYTHING to get your mind off of what has happened. You spend ONE more day like you have this past week and you're going to wind up in the Psycho Ward!!"

I didn't realize how right he was and I started to protest, but before I could say anything, our mess Sergeant, who was a buddy of mine, came into my office. (This was a set up, but I didn't know it until later!)

"Sergeant," the chaplain said. "Take Karl and get him out of here! Get him to do something or he's going to crack up!"

"Sure chaplain, I'll be glad to," the Sergeant replied. Turning to me and taking me by the arm he said, "C'mon Karl, let's go." As he pulled me out the door he said, "Let's go up to the Red Cross recreation room and play some ping-pong."

PLAY ping-pong??? THAT was the last thing I wanted to do! "I—I DON'T wanna play ping-pong," I growled.

"Just come on. You heard what the chaplain said."

After we got to the rec. room, I continued to balk and protest. "I DON'T WANT to play. I don't FEEL like playing!!"

Without a word, the Sergeant pushed me to the table, stuck a paddle in my hand, walked around to the other end of the table and started hitting the ball at me. There were other men around us in the room, and I didn't want to look like a complete idiot, so I began half-heartedly to hit the ball back to him. As the game proceeded, the Sergeant began to speed things up, and before I was aware of it, I was really into the game and found myself laughing and enjoying it! It was the first time in that whole week that I had laughed, and it broke the depression that had held me in its grip all week and had almost destroyed my mind. That evening I went to the mess hall and ate my first full meal in a week. The next morning, after a good night of sound sleep, I was back in the office, ready to work. My first job was one I didn't really care to do and which I could not have done during the past rugged week. I had the sad and difficult job of writing letters to each of the families and wives of the twenty-five men who were killed by that bomb. I made up the letters and typed them, and the chaplain read and signed them. I was very relieved when the last letter was in the mail. Those were the most difficult letters I've ever had to write.

A few days later, the Sergeant and another buddy went into town to see if they could find some fresh vegetables and fruit, which all of us were hungry for and missed very much. That evening the three of us, in my office, enjoyed fresh lettuce and fruit together. The chaplain had already gone for the day. Umm—mmm, was it ever good!! I hadn't had good fresh lettuce for soooo long. As I was chewing away, I felt something that felt a bit strange. I rolled it around with my tongue.

"Hmm, that feels like spaghetti," I thought. "But Nooo…wait a minute! I haven't HAD any spaghetti today AND we AREN'T eating any NOW. THIS AIN'T SPAGHETTI!!!" I immediately spit it out, and as soon as my buddies saw it, they burst out laughing. NONE of us ate any more lettuce that evening and none of us went into town to buy any more "fresh" vegetables with meat!! My "spaghetti" was a WORM—or what was left of it!!

Several days later, I went into downtown Liege. I don't remember what for, but I KNOW it was NOT for fresh veggies and meat! After I had been there for some time and it was getting late, I thought I'd better catch my streetcar and get back to the hospital. I made my way to the area where all the streetcars converged before heading out to the various parts of the city. There was a good-sized crowd of people waiting for their particular route. One after another, the cars stopped, loaded and went on their way. The crowd had gotten a lot smaller, and I was getting concerned, wondering if I had somehow missed my car, when it finally arrived; I was one of the last ones to get on. Just as I was stepping up onto the steps, someone came running up behind me. "Whew, I almost missed it!" he said with a loud gasp.

I turned to see who it was and recognized a fellow from our hospital. I had seen him several times, but we had never spoken to each other and didn't really know each other. Since the car was packed, we both stood holding on to the same pole. After introducing ourselves and standing silent for a few moments, Ernie suddenly looked at me.

"Karl, will you tell me something?" he asked. "I've been watching you. You're different from most of the other guys. You don't smoke, drink or do a lot of the things other guys do. You don't cuss and swear either. What is it that makes you different?"

WOW!! I was almost speechless! I had absolutely NO idea that he (or anyone else) was watching me like that! Talk about a jolt! WOW! It really made me do some serious thinking and praying in the following days, but what a great opportunity the Lord had given me to witness for Him!

I began telling him how I had accepted the Lord Jesus as my Lord and Savior when I was ten years old and since then I had no desire for those things because He had made a new creature out of me and filled me with His Peace and Joy. I no longer needed those things of this world. We talked all the way to our stop and as we walked the half-mile from the car stop to the hospital. When we got to the hospital, I assumed that he would go on to his tent. Instead, he went with me to the chaplain's office where we sat and talked until it was time to go to the mess hall for evening chow. He was so full of questions and had a real hunger for answers. We talked all the time we were eating and when we finished, we returned to the chaplain's office where we continued talking late into the night. He just didn't want to quit! How can you stop when someone is THAT hungry?? All of our talking was about the Lord and the Bible. We never once got off onto another subject. We became good buddies from then on and were together as often as possible. Whenever we were together, our conversation was mostly about the Lord. He just couldn't seem to get enough! How many times did I ask myself, "WHAT IF?" What if I had done ONE thing while he had been watching me that was wrong or un-Christlike?? Not that I was perfect by any means. The Lord knows I sure wasn't. We just never know who is watching, do we??

(Note: Ernie and I lost track of each other after I was transferred out of the 76th General Hospital to another outfit— beginning my long journey home. I really felt bad. It was several years after I got home and had almost given up hope that I finally located him and contact was established. We wrote to each other regularly after that hoping that one day we could get together for a visit, but sadly, it never happened. Early in 2003, Ernie passed away after a long illness. I regret to say that I cannot positively say that Ernie ever accepted Jesus as his Savior. I can only hope and pray that he did. Although we talked and talked and even prayed together, he never came right out and said that he had accepted the Lord into his heart and life. God said His Word would NOT return to Him void. With His help, I sure planted it in Ernie's heart.)

Two weeks later, the weather had warmed up enough to melt much of the snow and ice. As a result, the tent had dried out and was sagging badly, so I went out to tighten the ropes before it fell in on us completely. I started at the left side of the door and proceeded working around the tent, tightening the rope as I went. When I reached the last rope just outside the right side of the door, I came to a complete stop and froze. I saw something imbedded in the very middle of the walk about eighteen inches in front of the door. Curious, I began to dig and pry it loose, as it was firmly imbedded in the gravel of the walk, which was not yet completely thawed out. I finally got it loose after a lot of effort and held in my hand a good-sized piece of twisted, sharp-edged metal. It was a chunk of that bomb! As I stood staring at that piece of metal, reality began to set in. I remembered how I ran to the door to go out, but COULD NOT because it was as if someone was blocking the door keeping me from going out. I remembered that the second I stopped I had heard something hit the ground just outside the door. By this time there were tears in my eyes as the realization of what had happened fully dawned on me. Aloud, I said, "Thank you, Jesus."

I was too overwhelmed to say anymore. I KNEW (and I KNOW today) that it was the Lord or an angel that stood in that doorway and kept me from going out. IF I had stepped out that door at that moment, THAT chunk of bomb that I was holding in my hand would have hit me on the top of my head and I would not be here today!! As deeply as that was imbedded in that frozen, gravel walk, it would have gone halfway through my head, killing me instantly! Again, twice in one day the Lord kept the devil from destroying me, but as we shall see, the old devil wasn't through trying!!

There was, however, one more part of this story. A VERY important part! That bomb hit our hospital shortly after 8 A.M. on January 8, 1945. On February 8, one month later, I received a letter from my mother, written JANUARY 8. The first words of her letter were "Is something wrong? Are you in danger? I was awakened a little before 2 A.M. and I felt I had to pray for you."

The time difference between Belgium and America is SIX hours!! When she was praying at 2 A.M. in Ohio, it was 8 A.M. in Belgium where I was!! I sure am glad that there is NO distance in prayer! The Lord doesn't do things halfway, does HE??

Soon after this, I received a welcome break. Since the fighting had passed through the area where my grandparents (my Dad's parents) lived, I was granted permission to go into Germany and visit them. However, besides the jeep driver and myself, I had to have an officer with me in case there were any problems. This was a 600-mile round trip. As we passed through many towns and villages, I could hardly believe the total, awful destruction. Towns completely flattened—nothing but piles of brick and rubble. Believe me, there is absolutely nothing glamorous or adventurous about war. We passed through the city of Heilbronn, which had a population of 60,000 people and which had been heavily bombed. There was not one building that we could see with a second floor on it! One bomb shelter had about 300 people in it. A bomb hit it in such a way that it sealed the shelter shut making a tomb for everyone in it. What was to have been a refuge became a tomb instead. Over 30,000 people, half of the city, died that night. Heilbronn was twenty-five miles from the village where my grandparents lived. My grandmother told me that they could see the flames of the burning city. One of my aunts who lived there, told me how she wrapped wet blankets around herself and ran through the flames and managed to get out of the city.

When we arrived in the village of Mainhardt (mine-hart) where my grandparents lived, I told the officer with me that we would have to stop at the Post Office to get directions. I knew that they lived just outside of the village, but I couldn't remember exactly how to get there. After all, I was only nine years old when I was there in 1934, which of course was the last time they had seen me. Things can change a lot in eleven years. We finally located the Post Office, and while the others waited for me in the jeep, I went in to inquire. The jeep itself attracted a lot of attention because of what was on the front of it just below the windshield. Painted in big, white letters was the word "CHAPLAIN" with white crosses on each side of it. I was using the chaplain's jeep. I guess they thought I was the chaplain!!

Once inside the Post Office, I found myself in a small room with absolutely no one in sight! Now what was I going to do? Then I spied what I assumed was a doorbell on one wall. I stood there for a moment and debated whether or not I should press it since I didn't know what to expect. Would I blow the place up?? I finally gave it a quick poke and heard a bell ringing somewhere above me. When I heard someone calling, I stepped out the door and looking up saw a woman leaning out a window. Her face was a picture of alarm and fear. She had seen the jeep, the officer and the driver, who by this time were surrounded by a crowd of curious people. The people in the crowd were getting nowhere because they spoke no English and those in the jeep didn't speak German. When the woman above saw ME step out the door she REALLY was scared. After all, it had only been several days before when American troops had fought through their village and the military government had just arrived to set up their offices and take control the day before!! These people just didn't know what to expect, especially since the Nazis had drilled into them that the Americans would be cruel and would torture them, take away their food (which they didn't have too much of anyway) and take away their homes before killing them. No wonder they were frightened when they saw us American monsters!! It's understandable when you consider that they had lived twelve years in what was anything but a "paradise," living in constant fear of being betrayed by neighbors and people that they thought they could trust, reported to the Gestapo over some innocent or joking remark that they might have made. They never knew when the Gestapo or Hitler's "elite" Storm Troopers might break into their home and haul them off to a Concentration Camp.

In a very shaky voice, the woman asked me, in German of course, what I wanted. She was surprised when I answered her in German, and it made her relax a little. I explained to her that I was trying to find the way to my grandparent's house. Just then, a woman across the street leaned out her window and the two began talking back and forth. From the gist of their conversation, I concluded that they couldn't help me, so I returned to the jeep, hoping that someone in that crowd could give me the information I needed. There was one spunky, little old man who seemed to be the spokesman for the whole crowd. He stepped forward and asked if he could help. He had heard me speaking German to the woman in the window, so he knew that I spoke his language. I explained to him why I was there and gave him my grandparent's name. After some discussion with others in the crowd, he informed me that none of them knew of anyone in the village by that name!! I was beginning to get shook up and desperate, and the officer with me was getting impatient.

"Hurry up and do something," he ordered disgustedly. He thought I was getting too friendly with these "enemies."

Just then, the little old man that I had been talking to turned to one of the others and said, "I wonder if that could be in the Baad (bod)—there is a family by that name down there."

WHEN he said that, bells began ringing in my head. I suddenly remembered when my Dad wrote home to his mother, he always addressed it "Baad Mainhardt." This whole area had at one time been known for its hot springs and mineral baths where people from all over came to bathe for health reasons. That is how the area got its name "Baad," which means "bath" in German. "YES, YES," I said all excited. "THAT'S who I am looking for, that's where they live!!"

Immediately the little man said, "If it's alright, I'll ride with you and show you the way."

I think he wanted to ride in the American jeep more than anything else!! After checking with the officer and receiving his grudging approval, we piled into the jeep and were soon on our way leaving the rest of the crowd standing in the street. Believe me, I was really getting excited, but my excitement was somewhat dampened when the man told me that my grandfather had passed away in 1944.

We had no way of knowing, since there was no mail service between Germany and America because of the war.

As we drove down the street following the man's directions, I saw a woman with two little girls in the yard of a house on the left side of the street. Just as we were almost even with them, the man yelled, "Halt! Halt!"

Hearing the man, whom she obviously knew, yelling as we came to a screeching stop, her face filled with alarm and fear. I thought she might turn and run into the house. She was even more frightened when the man jumped out of the jeep, ran around to her side of the jeep and called to her. "Come here! Come here!" he said, motioning for her to come.

By this time, I had climbed out of the jeep and was standing beside the man. I had recognized the woman at once as one of my six aunts, however, I let the man handle things, although it was very hard to keep quiet! Slowly, she approached the jeep with both little girls clinging close to her. She stopped about six feet in front of us, looking from the man to me. Pointing to me, the man asked, "Do you know who this is?"

"How should I know who he is?" she asked fearfully, all the while staring at me, but showing no signs of recognition.

"Your brother who lives in America," he answered, "this is his son."

"ACH," she responded, her eyes fastened on me, "don't kid around with me."

I couldn't keep quiet any longer. Stepping forward, I said, "Tante (Aunt) Elsa, he's not kidding!"

With that, she lunged toward me, grabbing me in a big bear hug, saying over and over, "I can't believe it—I can't believe it—It just can't be possible!!" After recovering from her shock, she asked, "Have you seen Grandma yet?"

"No," I answered, "we're on our way there now."

"Then I'll go with you if it's alright," she said as she started toward the jeep.

Then she, her two girls and I climbed into the jeep and took off, leaving the little man standing there in the street! In all the excitement, it never occurred to me to get his name or to thank him for his help. Everything just happened so fast. I'm sure he would have liked to go along and see my grandmother's reactions when she saw me, but there just wasn't any room in the jeep, even though he was little!

Soon after we left the village, the road went downhill for a long distance as grandma's house was in a deep, beautiful valley. The "road" was a gravel lane, a bit rough in places, but passable. Very few cars ever used it, so when a car did come down it, everyone in the house would run to the windows to see who was coming. That's why there was someone in almost every window as we approached the house. At once we could see fear and apprehension on their faces as soon as they saw the American Army jeep and three American soldiers. When they saw my aunt and her two girls in the jeep too, they really got shook up. As soon as we came to a stop in front of the house, I jumped out of the jeep to go around to the other side. When I got there, everyone who had been looking out of the windows moments before were all standing in a half circle around the jeep. How they got down there so fast, I'll never know, but there they were—my five other aunts and their children, a cousin—and my grandmother! Once she looked at me she never took her eyes off me. I think that she thought she recognized me, but just wasn't sure. It was as if she knew who I was, but was too shocked to believe it. The aunt, Elsa, who had ridden down with us began to explain what was going on, letting them know that there was nothing to be afraid of. Then she finally told them who I was. At that, grandma, with a little cry, came and threw her arms around me. What a reunion that was!!

The officer and our driver returned to the village, where they found a place to stay with the military government. I spent three very wonderful days visiting with my grandmother and six aunts and getting to know the cousins I had never seen. One day my grandmother and I visited the cemetery and my grandfather's grave. It was a sad moment for me because I had loved my grandpa very much. Poor grandma!! First, she lost her husband, then in the following years of the war, she lost two sons and two sons-in-law in Russia. When I was there, she had one son-in-law who was still a prisoner-of-war in Russia. When he finally came home, he was just a shell of a human being, unable to work and barely alive. Grandma told me that when the fighting was going on around their village and their house that she, my aunts, one with five small children, and a cousin all huddled together in their basement, a cold, dark, damp room with no windows, for three days and nights. I had been in that basement and believe me, I WOULD NOT want to spend even ONE hour in there!!!

When I got back to our hospital, I wrote to my parents (a very difficult letter to write), telling them about my trip, my visit with my grandmother, my aunts and my cousins, and of course, the sad news too. Since the war had disrupted all mail services, my Dad had no way of knowing about the loss of his dad and two brothers. It was quite a shock for him. I had taken pictures of his mother and sisters with their children and was able to send pictures home.

Sadly, it was too short a time and as usual, all good things must come to an end. In no time, it seemed, we were saying sad "good-byes" (are there ever any really glad ones??) and were on our way back to Belgium.

Just before I left Belgium to visit my grandmother, one of the prisoners came to me in the chaplain's office. He had heard that I was going into Germany and he wanted to know if I would deliver a letter for him. His parents lived not too far from where my grandmother lived, and he thought and was hoping that somehow, someone might get it to his parents. Since there was no mail service of any kind, I assured him that I would do what I could.

While I was visiting my grandmother, I learned that I had another uncle who had been discharged from the German Army for medical reasons and was the husband of the aunt we had met in the village. He came for a visit while I was there. As we talked, he told me that his job required him to travel to the city of Stuttgart, approximately forty miles away, several times a week. This was the city where the prisoner's parents lived!! I told my uncle about the prisoner and gave him the letter. It never once dawned on me that the prisoner's last name and my uncle's was the same!! When he looked at the envelope and saw the name and address, the expression on his face was a mixture of surprise and shock. "Do you know who this prisoner is?" he asked.

"No," I answered. "I just know that he's an eighteen-year old German boy."

"Well," he responded, "you and he are related!!"

He then proceeded to explain our relationship, which was on his side of the family. Imagine the boy's surprise when I told him that he and I were related. From that day on, he made sure that every prisoner in that camp knew that I was his relative and he was mine!!

Piece of Buzz Bomb shrapnel found outside my tent.

X
PEACE AT LAST!!

May 8, 1945…V.E. Day…VICTORY IN EUROPE!!

The day that everyone had been praying and waiting for was finally here! The first thing I did when I entered the office that morning was turn on the radio, just in time to hear General Eisenhower announce that Germany had surrendered. The war in Europe was OVER!! I dropped to my knees and with tears of joy, praised the Lord for bringing me safely through it all. As I knelt there praying, I heard church bells ringing all over the city of Liege. Soon, every bell that people could get their hands on was ringing everywhere. WHAT a beautiful sound!! What a contrast from "buzz bombs" and thousands of bombers flying over day after day. It was almost too quiet!!

NOW, our main concern and the topic of every conversation was, WHEN and HOW SOON were we going home?? It couldn't be soon enough as far as I was concerned!!

Finally, a few months later, the day we were all waiting for arrived. On our last Sunday in Liege, I conducted the final service for the prisoners, not in the stockade, but in our own chapel, which they had built! I had to do some real hard talking, but I finally managed to work it out. The prisoners were all really amazed that we would allow THEM to come into OUR chapel and have a service there. What a service it was!! Such singing! Maybe it sounded better because it was in our chapel! Although they knew it was the last service and the sadness of parting was coming, they sang every hymn with all their hearts. They sang my favorite hymn especially for me (it was theirs, too) with special feeling. It was one we sang at every service.

So nimm den meine Hände und fünre mich,
So take then my hands and guide me,

bis an mein selig Ende und Ewiglich,
until my blessed and eternal end,

Ich will allein nicht gehen, nicht einen Shritt
I do not want to walk alone, not one step,

Wo Du wirst gehen und stehen, da—nimm mich mit.
Where You go and stand (stay), there—take me along.

It is still a favorite hymn and prayer of mine today.

They knew how much I enjoyed their singing and just didn't want me to forget. I knew as I looked into their faces that I would never see many of them again on this earth and THAT made it difficult for me to speak that evening. I managed to get through it and VERY reluctantly, brought the service to a close. Then, the prisoners took over for a short time before returning to the stockade. One by one, they stood and expressed their thanks, their appreciation for the services every Sunday night and for the kindness and love I had shown them. I had made their days as prisoners-of-war much easier and bearable for them. They all spoke with difficulty, trying hard to hold back their tears. You can imagine what I was doing! I was having a hard time holding back my own tears!! Then different ones presented me with little things they had made for me out of odds and ends they found in the stockade. One had embroidered a motto on a large piece of cloth. Another had painted a large framed picture of Jesus praying in the Garden of Gethsemane, (he had also made the frame). Another found a piece of aluminum from a plane that had been shot down, and taking a piece from the handle of a toothbrush, he made a beautiful ring for me. It was with a sad, yet full and thankful heart that I watched those prisoners leave that chapel, each one turning to wave to me, weeping as they went out the door. What really made me feel proud of them was the fact that ALL fifty or sixty of them marched the half-mile FROM the stockade to the chapel and after the service BACK to the stockade WITHOUT ANY GUARDS!!! The whole bunch of them could have taken off, but none of them did! They even had to pass a large cemetery on one side of the road, which would have given them some excellent temporary hiding places. Even those in charge of the stockade were amazed. They couldn't believe it!! Those prisoners KNEW that I trusted them and weren't about to let me down...and they DIDN'T!!

All of our time there in Liege was not devoted entirely to caring for patients and dodging "buzz bombs," or in my case, serving as the Chaplain's assistant and running errands for him. We were able to visit in the homes of some of the people, which was very interesting and very enjoyable in spite of the language problem. Most of us spoke no French and they spoke no English. In the end, we had a lot of good laughs, both them and us, trying to communicate with each other! This is how we met eleven-year old Marcel and ten-year old Andrea. They each came from separate families. Each one of their fathers had been executed by the Nazis because they were active in the Underground movement working against the Nazis. When our Christian group and the chaplain heard this, we wanted to do something to help them. We invited them to come to our hospital and visit with us and join us for meals. They enjoyed this very much since they didn't have much to eat at home, and of course, eating

American food (even if it was Army chow!!) was a real treat for them. They were a little timid at first, but it didn't take them long to relax and fit right in. Soon after they started coming as our regular "guests," we "adopted" them and made Marcel and Andrea the "Mascots" of the 76th General Hospital!! They were truly two great, wonderful kids and bright spots in our lives. We always looked forward to their visits and tried to have them as often as possible. After we left Liege, we lost track of them. I wrote to Marcel after I got home, but the letter came back marked "Unknown." I don't know if any of the other guys ever tried to locate them or not. At least those that I have corresponded with over the years never did. Sadly, we just don't know what happened to our two little "Mascots"!

When we finally left Liege, we turned the hospital over to another outfit and moved to Antwerp, a seaport in northern Belgium. Was this our first step on the road home?? After all, this was a SEAPORT! Little did I know that there would be many more stops to come before I would finally get home. I guess it's a good thing I DIDN'T know!! By this time, I should have known how the Army operates. They sure were in a big hurry to get me over there, but it seemed (to me) as if they were taking their good old summer time to get me back home!!

Now, we had a new language to contend with, Flemish, which is a combination of French, Dutch and German. This was the language spoken in the northern-half of Belgium. Whatever, we still couldn't understand it!!

One evening one of their streetcars plowed into one of our Army trucks at the entrance to the building where we were living. Since it was on a main thoroughfare, there was a lot of traffic. So, trying to be helpful, I went out on one side of the accident and stopped traffic and tried to tell them to go around the accident...SLOWLY. They just looked at me and went zooming on their way. I finally got disgusted and decided I would try German whether they liked it or not. There was still a lot of hatred for anything German. The next car I stopped, I motioned from them to go around the accident and then loudly said, "LANGSAM," (German for "slowly"), and it worked!! No problem from then on!

The building we lived in had been a hospital operated by Catholic nuns. We were not operating a hospital anymore and would never again. We were just an outfit waiting to go home, although we were still called the 76th General Hospital.

While I was there in Antwerp, I was sent on an errand to the city of Charleroi in southern Belgium, which was about seventy-five miles from Antwerp. My buddy, Chalmert, drove the jeep and two guys went with us. I don't recall why they came along, but there were four of us in the jeep. The highway we traveled on was excellent compared to many other roads that had bore the brunt of fighting and military traffic. Along the right side of the highway was what appeared to be a sidewalk, but most of the people, young and old, rode bicycles, so this "sidewalk" was actually a bikeway. We were clipping along at a good rate of speed on a long, straight stretch of highway, when we saw a boy on a bicycle some distance ahead of us going the same direction we were. Just as we drew almost even with him, he suddenly turned left directly in front of us! He was trying to cross the highway to a lane on the left side that no doubt led to the farmhouse where he lived. He never once turned to look before turning out onto the highway. This was a busy, main highway. You would have thought that he would have had enough sense to look before turning out onto the highway. HOW we ever missed him, I will never know, but thankfully we did. However, in swerving to avoid hitting the boy, the driver lost control of the jeep. For some distance, we rode on the edge of the road, struggling to keep from going into the ditch. He almost had the jeep back on the road when we hit a small mound of dirt and tipped over into the ditch onto the driver's side. Shaken, but unhurt, except for a few bumps and bruises, we climbed out of the jeep. The first thing we did was thank the Lord that we hadn't hit that boy and that He had kept us from any serious injuries. Then, we looked for the boy. He was nowhere to be seen and neither was his bicycle, so we assumed that he was okay. He probably made one fast beeline up that lane to his house as fast as he could pedal. I'm sure he was probably as scared as we were!

Shortly after, a British Army truck stopped and several soldiers climbed out. After finding out what happened and sizing-up the situation, they had the jeep back on all four wheels in short order, and we were on our way again. After that, every time our driver saw ANYONE on a bicycle, for some reason he would blow the horn until we were past them!! They were probably wondering what in the world was the matter with these crazy Americans!! As we traveled on to Charleroi, I knew in my own heart that once again, the Lord had kept me from yet another attempt by the devil to destroy me, but that old rascal the devil wasn't through trying yet!! The rest of our trip to Charleroi and back to Antwerp was uneventful.

Soon after my return to Antwerp, I received a blow to my hopes of getting home soon. I wasn't going back to the States with my own outfit, the 76th General Hospital. I was transferred to the 160th Station Hospital in Charleroi from where I had just returned! I was there for a little over a month. While there, I met another boy who was also a Christian and a member of the Assemblies of God as I was. We were both overjoyed when we located an Assemblies of God church right there in Charleroi! Of course we went to every service we could. Although we couldn't understand anything, since neither of us spoke French, we felt right at home when we heard them singing the same old hymns we sang at home—they in French and the two of us in English!! A few people spoke some English, including the Assistant Pastor, who spoke very fluent English. I was really surprised when they asked me to speak in the Sunday evening service. I had never preached through an interpreter before, so it proved to be quite an experience. The Assistant Pastor interpreted, and with the Lord's help, everything went very well. It wasn't easy though, so the

Lord HAD to help me. I sure don't know what I would have done without Him!

We met a young man in his twenties who had spent some time in a Nazi labor camp. He was really nice and so were his parents and sister. It was just too bad that we couldn't talk to each other because of the language barrier. We did enjoy a couple of wonderful "international" dinners in the Pastor's home. They were "international" because there were foods from many different countries. I don't know where or how he got it all so soon after the war ended, but I KNOW it sure was good!! It was a real treat for both of us. These wonderful people really made our stay in Charleroi a very pleasant memory, but as usual in the Army, another change was coming. It was getting so that I never knew where I was going to be from one day to the next!

I was transferred again to a medical detachment in the 89th Infantry Division at Camp Twenty Grand near Rouen, France. This was a staging area for troops that were on their way home. At last, I was making some progress toward getting home, I thought, but as it turned out, Camp Twenty Grand was to be my "home" for almost a month!! Although I was anxious to get home, our time at Twenty Grand was actually a pleasant time.

As we were going through the chow line on our first day there, I was surprised to see German prisoners working in the kitchen and serving us our food. Because I'd had enough of being called a "Nazi lover" and a lot of other unpleasant things, I decided that I would not let on that I understood or spoke German. THAT decision lasted until the next day! As we were going through the line the next day, I came to the prisoner, a young boy, who was handing out the bread. He was having an awful time trying to ask each one how many slices they wanted. When I got to him, I felt sorry for him (soft-hearted me!!) and forgot all about my resolve of the day before. I held up two fingers and said "zwei" (two).

THAT did it!! He got all excited and yelled as loud as he could, "Ach, Sie sprechen Deutsch!!" (Oh, you speak German!!)

The eyes of every prisoner in that service line and even in the kitchen turned toward me! I was a marked man!! "Oh no," I thought. "What have I done? I really blew it now." However, things turned out to my advantage! From that moment on, I received larger portions of everything every time I came through the line: especially any desserts!!

Later that day, one of the prisoners, a twenty-year old named Heinz, came to my tent and asked if he could do our laundry for us; an offer we gladly accepted since we had no laundry facilities. (We paid the prisoners with Hershey bars, candy bars, or anything we had to give away, and they were glad to get whatever they got.) A few mornings later, Heinz who worked the early-morning shift in the kitchen, came into our tent, over to my cot and woke me up. He proceeded to tell me what there was for breakfast that morning. He did this each morning from then on until we left Camp Twenty Grand. If the breakfast was pancakes or fresh eggs, which wasn't often, we all got up and went to breakfast. If it was anything else, we stayed in bed and Heinz would come back with a large pot of hot coffee. He would come to each of our cots and fill our canteen cups with hot coffee. Many times he would bring other tidbits of things left over from breakfast that he thought we would like. What a life!! We were living the life of Riley!! Of course the rest of the fellows in the tent didn't mind that one bit!! At least NONE of them called me a Nazi lover!!

One thing we had at Twenty Grand was plenty of time. Since we had no duties to perform, no marching and drilling (thank goodness!) and NO smart aleck officers to dream up ridiculous things for us to do, our time was our own. This gave me plenty of time to play my violin, which I had carried with me all during my time in the Army. Heinz, when he was free, would often come to the tent, sit on the floor and listen to me play. After the first time he told me that there was a violin in the camp, a Stradivarius! He thought sure that he could get it for me! WOW!! A Stradivarius!! I could hardly believe it. Imagine my disappointment and anger when Heinz came to me a few days later and very reluctantly told me that some American soldier had found the violin and not knowing the value of the instrument, had playfully smashed it over another guy's head!!! It was a good thing I didn't know who the guy was, because I would surely have clobbered HIM!! At least, I sure felt like it. It isn't every day that you can get your hands on a genuine Stradivarius violin. I had no reason to believe that Heinz was anything but honest with me.

As the day of our departure approached, we began going through our stuff, getting rid of as many things as possible. We didn't want to lug anything more home than we had to. What did we do with all the stuff we were getting rid of? We gave it to the prisoners who had been so nice to us. They were so thankful for everything they were given. I gave Heinz my dress shoes since I would be getting new ones after I got home. Why should I lug this pair all the way home?? He didn't want to take them at first; he just couldn't believe I was actually GIVING them to him. You should have seen him when he finally realized that I WANTED him to have them. You would have thought that I had given him two bars of gold!!

On the last night there, Heinz came to our tent. I happened to be alone just then. We chatted for a short time and after we had exchanged home addresses, we proceeded to say our good-byes. When we couldn't think of any more to say, we just stood in silence looking at each other. Suddenly, Heinz broke down and began to sob like a baby. My own eyes weren't exactly dry either. We were delaying the inevitable as long as we could. Finally, after saying a final "good-bye," Heinz turned, still crying, and left the tent—not knowing if we would ever see each other again.

Once again, as the saying goes, "All good things must come to an end," and that time had come again. I'm sure that if it wasn't that we all were anxious to get home, we would just as soon stay there and continue living the life of Riley!

Note--In 1973, I had the privilege to travel to Germany, where I spent two wonderful weeks visiting Heinz, his wife and three beautiful daughters. Heinz's kindness to me in Camp Twenty Grand carried over into his home twenty-eight years later!!

One Saturday morning, we were all ordered to fall into formation with ALL our equipment. Oh boy!! We're finally on our way!! By this time we were a "packet" of men, no longer an outfit of any kind, consisting of fifteen men who were scheduled to go to Indian Town Gap, Pennsylvania, to be discharged. As we stood in formation, the officer in charge called us to attention. "ALL of you men who are to be discharged from Indian Town Gap in Pennsylvania, fall out with your gear and return to your tent."

We were stunned!! WHY?? WHY US?? WHAT was going on??? Very slowly we picked up our gear and returned to our tent, but not before we watched all the other men climb into the trucks headed for seaport—and home. We sat in a daze, trying to figure out what was going on. We soon found out, and when we did, our shock and bitter disappointment turned to anger and outrage. It seems the colonel in some outfit had some work that needed to be done that HE considered very important, so he promised his men that if they got it done by a certain time, he would see to it that they got to go home sooner!! Guess how many men were involved??? FIFTEEN!!! THEY finished the work, and WE got bumped out and replaced by his men. We heard later that they, and the original group we should have gone with, went home on a Liberty ship headed for Newport News, Virginia. Liberty ships were small, freighter-like ships used to transport military equipment such as trucks, tanks and ammunition. They were a far cry from being luxury liners!! Hmmm, maybe this was a break for us!

That night at 2 A.M., we were awakened, told to get all our gear together (huh, as if any of us had unpacked anything!!) and told to be ready to leave. (We had been ready for the last six months!!) We were immediately loaded into an OPEN semi-trailer truck like a bunch of cattle and were FINALLY on our way. This was in the middle of November and it was freezing cold. Riding twenty-five miles in an open semi was definitely no pleasure cruise! Now I know what Eskimos must feel like. We huddled together as much as we could, trying to keep warm, but it didn't help a whole lot. When we arrived at our destination, some of the guys jumped down off the truck and then fell to the ground in pain because their feet were so cold and numb. Seeing this, the rest of us climbed down VERY slowly and carefully.

After we had what was SUPPOSED to be hot coffee and stale Red Cross donuts, we were hustled onto a ferryboat used to ferry railroad cars across the English Channel between France and England. One end of the ferryboat was wide open, so they hung a huge tarpaulin over it to keep the cold wind out. It sure didn't keep the cold out!! There was no heat at all, no sleeping facilities, no kitchen to prepare any meals of any kind, and of course, no place to eat meals, but then, we were only supposed to be on this thing two or three hours!! There were several other outfits on board besides the fifteen of us, altogether about 300 men.

By this time, it was daylight, and we were SUPPOSED to leave for Southampton, England, shortly after daybreak, BUT we didn't move! We were all anxious and impatient to get underway so that we could get off that miserable boat as soon as possible. You can imagine our disgust and anger when we learned the reason for the delay. Typical Army foul-ups!! Another outfit was supposed to come on board after us, but they were unable to get transportation, so we had to wait for them!! WE sat there all that day and all the next night with only cold C-Rations to eat (to which I was allergic!), freezing and with no place to sleep. Some of the guys huddled together trying to get warm. Ordinarily, we would have had a blanket with us, but those had been turned in before we left Camp Twenty Grand. We weren't SUPPOSED to need them anymore!! HA!

Early the next morning, the "missing" outfit finally arrived, and soon after, we were on our way to Southampton—at last!! The distance was only thirty miles, and it took us four hours since we didn't have to zig and zag our way across this time. As we were entering the harbor of Southampton, we saw a large ship just leaving the harbor—headed for New York. Before the war, that ship had been the German luxury liner "Europa." It had been taken over by the U.S. and used as a troop transport. WE were supposed to be on THAT ship!! The one-day delay had caused us to miss that ship. Hooo-boy, WHAT next??? Was I EVER going to get home??

By the time we docked and got off that miserable ferry, it was getting dark. We were loaded onto a train and after about an hour delay, we were taken to a small out-of-the-way place about thirty-five miles north of Southampton. I never did find out the name of the place! It took us over four hours!! So much for the "speedy" British train service!!

We found ourselves shuffled into what had apparently been a small hotel at one time. Each room had a small fireplace in it as most British homes do, but there was no coal, wood or anything else to burn in them to help us keep warm. We were "parked" there to wait for a ship to take us to the U.S., and THAT is exactly what we did----- WAIT!!! There was absolutely nothing to do, and believe me, it gets mighty uncomfortable sitting around in the cold. As a result, when we left there two weeks later, there wasn't a cupboard door or any other wooden thing that was burnable in that place! We searched the grounds for anything that might burn, short of chopping down the trees that were around the place!! I guess no one thought about that, but none of us had an axe anyway, so it wouldn't have done any good. We'd probably have gotten into a lot of trouble if we had tried it. To top it off, we had to walk three or four blocks three times a day to where our mess tent was set up for our meals, and most of the time, it wasn't even worth the effort!!

After two weeks of this misery, we were back on the train again on our way to Southampton. Was THIS really IT or would there be more snafus and delays?? This time the train ride didn't take four hours, at least it didn't seem like it. As the train pulled into the harbor area, we saw a huge aircraft carrier at the dock—and it was American! Some of the guys started yelling, "LOOK, there's our ship!! WOW!!"

"Naw, we surely ain't going on something like THAT!!" some of the others responded.

I guess some of us had already had so many disappointments, we just couldn't believe that we could be THAT fortunate. Within a very short time, our train came to a stop; we got off the train and walked up the gangplank onto that aircraft carrier, the "U.S.S. ENTERPRISE"!!! She was known as the "Galloping Ghost" because the Japanese claimed to have sunk her SIX different times!! Soon after, we saw the cables that held the ship to the dock being cast off, felt the vibrations as the engines came to life and saw the space between the ship and the dock slowly widen as the ship backed slowly out into the harbor. At last, we were actually on our way, that is IF the ship didn't sink there in the harbor or some officer suddenly decided that we shouldn't be leaving yet!! After a short wait, the ship began moving forward, picking up speed and we were FINALLY on our way to New York City, where we scheduled to arrive in five days. Boy, this sure beat going home on a Liberty ship or even an old luxury liner!!

In a short time, we were out of the English Channel and into the Atlantic Ocean, where we immediately encountered stormy weather and rough seas. It continued to get worse the further we went. On the second night it got so bad that we turned around and headed back to Southampton all that night. I KNEW something had to happen to mess us up again!! We were unaware that we had turned around. We thought we were still on our way to New York. You know that when a ship as big as that aircraft carrier has to turn around because of the weather, it HAS to be pretty rough. Was there to be no end of delays?

Early on the morning of the third day, radio reports coming to the ship indicated that the storm had eased up, so we turned around again and started back to New York. At least NOW, we didn't have to worry about a convoy or submarines.

It was still plenty rough, but in spite of the stormy weather, I never missed a meal, although there were times when I thought my meals were going to miss ME!! Eating our meals proved to be a real experience, especially for a bunch of landlubbers like us! The tables were high enough so that we ate standing up. There weren't any chairs or benches to sit on anyway; that way you didn't linger too long at the table! We wondered why each table had a two-inch high slat of wood around the edges: we soon found out! As the ship pitched and rocked from one side to the other, we had to hold onto the table with one hand to keep from falling and at the same time, hold onto our tray with the other hand. If you didn't, your tray would suddenly slide to the other side of the table, and you had to wait for the ship to rock back the other way for your tray to come back to you!! THAT'S what those slats around the edges were for—to keep our tray from sliding off onto the floor. That's what I meant about my meals missing me! It really was something trying to grab a bite BEFORE your tray slid away from you again. It could take awhile to eat that way!! We had plenty of good laughs watching each other trying to eat. Maybe we should have grabbed a bite out of the other guy's tray when it came to us instead of waiting for our tray to come back!! One thing I was really thankful for was that I never got seasick. A lot of the guys were so seasick they couldn't even get out of their bunks. Even some of the sailors were sick!!

All in all, the Navy chow was pretty good, even the baked beans for BREAKFAST!! I heard about those beans for breakfast being an old Navy tradition, but I thought they were just kidding. Well, they weren't!! We had baked beans for breakfast, and I ATE'EM!! We held our noses a lot the rest of the day, too!! We were kinda sorry that we no longer had our gas masks!!

Since it was still stormy and rough, no one was allowed to go up on the flight deck, especially since there were no railings around the edge of the deck to keep anyone from being blown or washed overboard. Yes, some of the waves were high enough to come up onto the flight deck. We were still two days out of New York when the storm let up enough for us to be permitted to go onto the flight deck, which we all wanted to do very much. A sailor, whom my buddy and I had gotten acquainted with, offered to give us a tour of the ship; an offer we gladly and readily accepted. He took us all through the ship, even down into the engine room, which was fantastic and awesome. We ended up on the flight deck at the stern (back) of the ship. We looked forward and saw the prow of the ship rise high into the air and then plunge suddenly into a high wave. It looked as if the ship was going to take a nosedive straight to the bottom of the ocean! We watched in fascination as this was repeated over and over. We were approximately in the middle of the flight deck walking slowly toward the front of the ship, when suddenly, a very strong gust of wind hit us from the back, forcing us to run. We grabbed each other and tried hard to put on the brakes and stop running, but with the wind still blowing hard at our backs, it was very difficult. When we finally managed to stop, we were TWO feet from the edge of the flight deck! TWO feet away from going for a nice long swim. There was NO railings to keep us from going over the edge! The only problem was that I had not planned on doing any swimming that day! I didn't know how to swim anyway! Needless to say, we beat it back below deck as fast as we could, and for some reason, NONE of us had any further desire to go up on the flight deck again. Not the three of US anyway!! At least, NOT until we were able to see land and were approaching New York City.

Again, the devil had made one more attempt to destroy me, but again, the Lord had delivered me out of his hand!! I guess the devil is just a very slow learner!! He just doesn't know when to quit!!

It is impossible for me to describe my feelings as we entered the harbor of New York City, especially when we saw the Statue of Liberty standing straight and tall, welcoming us home. There was a lump in my throat as I stood there on the deck, thanking the Lord for bringing me safely through the war and home again and then thinking of those who weren't ever coming home again. In my mind's eye, I saw those cemeteries with rows and rows of little white crosses—the final resting places of those who gave their lives because of evil and wicked men.

Suddenly, there were tugboats all around our ship, blowing their whistles and shooting streams of water high into the air in a grand "WELCOME HOME" reception. As we slipped alongside the pier, we saw signs and banners everywhere saying "WELCOME HOME," and on the pier were hundreds of people cheering and waving flags—all that just to welcome ME home!!

The crossing from Southampton to New York should have taken five days. "You will be home in time for Christmas," they had promised us. Instead, because of the stormy weather, it took us nine days. We arrived in New York on December 24th, the day before Christmas! There was NO way that we could be discharged and get home in time for Christmas. NO WAY!! Some of those whose homes were near New York City were allowed to go home on pass for Christmas, but those who lived further away had to remain in Camp Kilmer, New Jersey, where we had been taken after getting off the ship. My buddy, whose home was in Pottstown, Pennsylvania, was able to go home and invited me to come to his home for Christmas. I was a little reluctant about going to the home of strangers, but I accepted and went with him. His family welcomed me and was very nice, but they and my buddy were not Christians, and before Christmas Day was over, I wished that I had stayed in camp. There was a lot of drinking, which I politely declined. I don't think my buddy would have made it back to camp Christmas night if I hadn't been there to help him on the train back to camp. It sure was anything but a Merry Christmas—for me anyway!

XI
THE LAST LAP

What a great feeling it was to be back on good old American soil again! As soon as we had gotten off the ship, we boarded a train for a very short train ride, which took us to Camp Kilmer in New Jersey. We were there two days during which time we turned in whatever equipment and Army stuff that we had left. Then, the fifteen of us who were scheduled for discharge at Indian Town Gap, Pennsylvania, were processed out and put on another train bound for our LAST stop before home. At Indian Town Gap things moved quickly, for a change, and on the 27th of December, all the guys in our group of fifteen were discharged and on their way home, EXCEPT ME!! WHAT next???

"We can't discharge you," I was told, "because all your Army records have been lost somewhere along the way. We'll have to make up a temporary record before we can discharge you."

Was I EVER going to get home?? Did the Army really want to keep me that bad?? Wow!! I was about ready to go AWOL!!

I spent a whole day giving them all the information they needed: all the places I had been from the day I entered the Army, the day I arrived and left those places, my duties as an orderly in the hospital and later as the chaplain's assistant, any promotions, awards or any battle ribbons and stars I was entitled to receive. What a lot of red tape just to get out of the Army so I could finally go home!!

FINALLY, on December 29, 1945, with my discharge safely tucked in my pocket, I climbed on the first train I could find that was headed for Dayton, Ohio. WOW!! I was still in uniform because that's all I had to wear, but I was no longer the property of Uncle Sam!! I was now a veteran and best of all—a CIVILIAN!!!!

I arrived in Dayton late in the afternoon, but I still wasn't "home." My parent's farm was eighty miles from Dayton, so I still had one more lap to go. I just needed to find a way to get there. I had an aunt and uncle living in Dayton. They were the only ones I could think of that would be able to help me, so I called them as soon as I got off the train. They came as soon as possible and picked me up. After visiting with them for a short time, they called another couple who were friends of our family. The man was my former violin teacher and had been a very good friend to me during my troubled and confused teenage years. They came at once to my uncle's house and after some lengthy discussion (too long as far as I was concerned!!), they arranged that they would all take me home. By this time, it was getting late, so my aunt suggested that maybe I should stay overnight, and they would take me home the next day! OH NO!! I wanted to get HOME!! Thankfully, the others came to my rescue!

"Oh no," they said, "he's been gone from home two and a half years and now that he's this close, he's SURELY anxious to get home as soon as possible to see his family."

After ALL the delays I had already had, I heartily and readily agreed with them!! I was only eighty miles away from home; I wasn't about to spend one more night away—even if I had to hitchhike or walk!!

After a lot of hustle and bustle, we all piled into the car and were soon on our way—at last! I could hardly believe it. THIS was actually the last LAP! As the miles passed by, I got more and more excited. Couldn't we go any faster?? Soon I was going to see my Mom and Dad, who at one time I thought I'd never see again on this earth, and I was going to see the little brother I had never seen! He had been born while I was in Paris. "What will be his reaction when he sees me?" went through my mind as we rode along. "Would he accept me as his older brother?" After all, I would be a complete stranger to him. I could hardly wait to find out.

It was 10:30 P.M. when we drove up in front of the house. The folks in the car remained in the car and allowed me to go to the door alone. I knocked on the door and it opened almost before I stopped knocking. They had heard the car coming up the lane and then stop in front of the house. Of course, they had no idea who was at the door since I had not let them know ahead of time when I was coming. How could I when I didn't know myself with all the delays, goof-ups and stormy weather!! As I had hoped, my Mom answered the door. Was this my Mom?? The mom who had brown hair when I left home was now completely white!! I couldn't believe it!! I didn't think I was THAT bad!! As soon as Mom saw me—well—I guess I don't have to describe what happened next!! What a welcome home THAT was!! It was even better than the one I received in New York City!!! There was, however, ONE exception. I was NOT welcomed by my little brother, Paul! He would have absolutely nothing to do with me! My parents, my other brother and my sister tried to explain to him that I was the guy whose picture (my Army picture) stood on top of the piano. He just shook his head, pointed to the picture and then to me and said, "NO-NO, THAT'S NOT HIM!!!"

It was almost six months before he would let me come near him. No matter what I said or did, he would start screaming if I came too close to him. I guess he could be excused though, because he wasn't quite one and half years old and he had never seen me before either. What a shock THAT must have been for him!!

On the day I was discharged, I weighed a trim 186 pounds. Within a few days after arriving home, I had Mom cooking all the good things I had missed for two and a half years and I guess I kinda made a pig out of myself!! It was a good thing (or was it??) that they lived on a farm and had a large herd of cows, because for the next few months I averaged at least a gallon of milk a day!! After all that powdered milk (we called it "chalk water"), I just couldn't get enough of the REAL thing!! No wonder that my weight jumped from 186 in December to 243 by the middle of March!! I can assure you that it didn't STAY that way for very long!! But then, who cares, I was celebrating and thanking the Lord, too, because at last I WAS FINALLY—HOME!!! Home sweet home!!

EPILOGUE

Remember Margaret in Portland, Oregon? The wonderful girl I met there, but couldn't think of getting serious with because I had a "girl" back home? Well, the "girl" back home couldn't wait for me as she had promised and she found another guy while I was overseas. She wrote me a "Dear John" letter, breaking our engagement. I was absolutely crushed! I felt that my world had come to an end. THAT, on top of all the other things I was going through at the time. My buddy, Chalmert, did everything he could think of to comfort me and cheer me up. I even questioned the Lord and found it hard to pray, but as usual, the Lord knew exactly what He was doing. He had started this and HE was going to finish it!! He dealt with me for the next few months until I said, "Okay Lord, YOUR will be done, but IF I ever get married, it's going to have to be the girl YOU give me!!"

Shortly after that, I received a letter from Margaret asking for an article for the Servicemen's section of their church paper. I responded and from then on, we began writing each other. In July of 1946, I went to Portland and visited with Margaret and her family. I had in mind proposing to her just before returning home two weeks later. She met me at the depot and walked right past me. She had never seen me in anything but my uniform and didn't even recognize me! I didn't let her get very far though!! On that first day, we decided to go to a beautiful park and then to the adjoining zoo to see the monkeys. As we walked through the park, I couldn't wait any longer. We found a nice bench, sat down and began to chat. We didn't chat very long before I said, "You have four other sisters don't you?"

"Well, yes," she said looking at me puzzled. "You know that I do."

"And you are the youngest, aren't you?" I asked.

"You know that I am." She was getting more and more puzzled, yet wondering where I was going with this conversation. She got even more puzzled when I asked the next question.

"None of them are married, are they?" I knew they weren't!

"Of course they're not. You know that!"

"Well, how about YOU being the first one?" There!! I had said it! THAT was my proposal!!

After a few moments of silence, she looked at me and said, "YES!!"

From there, we went into town to a jewelry store and looked at rings! We forgot all about seeing the monkeys! After all, it ain't everyday a guy gets engaged! At a time like that, who cares about monkeys anyway!! When I returned home two weeks later, we were officially engaged with her family's blessing!

In September of 1946, I entered North Central Bible Institute in Minneapolis, Minnesota, to begin training for the ministry. At the end of my first year, I returned to Portland and on June 21, 1947, we were married. In July of 1949, God blessed us with a wonderful son. We now have a grandson and a granddaughter. Now, after a little over fifty-five years of a wonderful and happy marriage, we give our Lord and our God praise and thanks for the way He has directed our lives!

DON'T
tell ME that
God's way isn't the best
WAY
EVEN if we don't understand it at the time! BELIEVE ME,

HE KNOWS

WHAT HE IS DOING IF WE'LL JUST LET HIM!!

MY PURPOSE

In writing this story, this part of my life, it is NOT for any glory for myself, but to give glory to Him Who made it all possible. If it were not for Him, I wouldn't be writing this—I wouldn't even be here. His love for a lonesome, homesick teenage soldier boy and His patience and longsuffering with the same stubborn teenager is why I am here today and able to tell this story. I don't enjoy telling some of the things that happened; the memories are still vivid and painful— even after fifty-seven years—but if whoever reads my story is blessed by it, helped by it and brought closer to my Jesus, I will feel that it was worth the pain of telling it.

ALL PRAISE, HONOR AND GLORY BELONG TO MY

WONDERFUL

LORD AND SAVIOR!!

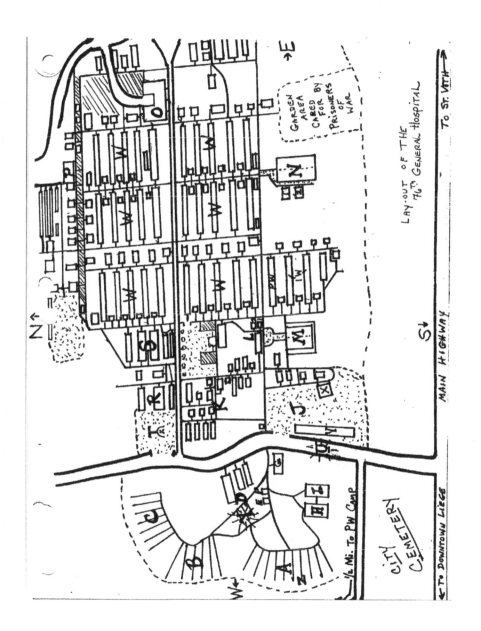

Lay-out of the
46th General Hospital

155

76th General Hospital

A—Enlisted Men's Quarters

B—Officer's Quarters

C—Nurse's Quarters

D—Laundry Unit

E—Post Office

F—Company Office

G—Supply

H—Mess Tent

I—Kitchen

J—Motor Pool

K—Clinics and Headquarters Offices

L—Old Chapel

    1—Protestant

    2—Catholic (Chaplain's Offices)

M—Theater

N—New Chapel

    1—Protestant

    2—Catholic (Chaplain's Offices)

O—P.X. (Post Exchange)

P—Morgue

R—Receiving and Admitting

S—Surgery

T—Monument (Memorial to twenty-five men killed by 2nd bomb)

V—Garage

W—Wards

    PW—Psycho Ward

    IW—Isolation Wards

X—Motor Pool Office

U—1st Buzz Bomb Hit

Y—2nd Buzz Bomb Hit

Z—My Tent

FINISHING THE RACE

In the epilogue, the author, our grandfather, alluded to the month and year being February 2004. Since then, much has changed. In September of that year, Karl and Margaret's only son and our father, Donald Feucht, passed away from advanced colon cancer. Although it has brought the family closer together, the loss would profoundly affect both of our grandparents. We know neither of them ever thought they'd outlive their only child. During this time, everyone in the family had to rely on God and trust in His sovereignty. We do believe, however, that losing our father has made us into stronger individuals with much deeper faiths.

Knowing and trusting in God's goodness and believing in His promises to us, our grief, though difficult at times, eventually subsided and day-to-day living began to feel more normal. In addition, a few years after the loss of Don, a blessing arrived to our grandparents in the form of a great-grandson, born to Karl, and his beautiful wife, Kristen. For our grandparents, becoming great-grandparents was truly a joy. Grandpa wouldn't hesitate to point out that not only were they "grand," but now they were also "great." Two more great-grandchildren arrived and, although living several hours away, the time spent together enriched Karl and Margaret's lives.

As the years passed and a new family was formed, Grandpa's health began to fade and what was once normal and considered easy became difficult and challenging. Plagued by neuropathy and a frailty no one had seen in him before, we knew each visit back home might be one of the last ones that we'd have to spend time with Grandpa. It was in October of 2013 when Grandpa suffered a mini-stroke. He was taken to the hospital and after a few days was moved into a skilled nursing facility, yet was also suffering from aspiration pneumonia, requiring a tube for nutrition. On November 17, 2013, Karl J. Feucht, our grandfather, left his earthly residence to begin his eternal life in heaven with the Lord. We couldn't help thinking immediately of our father greeting Grandpa into heaven and the two of them sharing in a joyful reunion. What a wonderful, indescribable gift we have in God's endowment of eternal life and the promise to live with Him forever, being reunited with those that have gone before us.

Preceding Grandpa in death was his brother, David, who passed in April of 2010. He is survived by a sister, Esther, living nearby; a brother, Paul, living in Florida; and a daughter-in-law,

Rosemary, who lives in the same small town that Karl and Margaret have called home for nearly thirty years.

Margaret, or as we have always called her, "Nani," continues to live at home and continues to be blessed with good health. She receives frequent visits from neighbors, and a couple of college girls come by regularly to visit and play a family favorite: Skip-Bo. An additional blessing is that Esther and her son, Grandpa's nephew, Randy, visit often and offer assistance wherever needed. A fourth great-grandchild will be arriving soon, bringing yet another wonderful blessing.

Grandpa's love for his family was evident. We rarely saw him angry, heard him raise his voice, or become impatient. In fact, growing up, the only times we can remember him showing any visibility of irritation was when he was dealt a bad hand in Skip-Bo or just could not manage to play the top card on his deck! Every New Year's Day he would spoil the family by preparing a delicious meal of pork, cabbage rolls, sauerkraut, spaetzle, and gravy. Standing on the front porch and waiting to come inside, we could smell the appetizing aroma from the kitchen of the traditional German dinner. Another way Grandpa showed his love for his family and others was through his artistic side. Grandpa would create memorable poems every Christmas and mail them out to many friends, relatives, and acquaintances. He always took time to write a card and carefully inscribe the names on the envelopes, rarely forgetting a birthday or anniversary. But perhaps the most cherished of his works of art would be cartoons that he would illustrate and narrate. Particularly precious to Karl, in a time before email, cell phones, and text messaging, Grandpa would create cartoon drawings for his then-preschool-aged grandson and mail them overseas to Germany when Karl, Don, and Rosemary were living there for several years.

Our grandparents were married for 66 years before our grandpa's death. Their example of a loving, sacrificial, and Christ-led marriage is something we cherish and aim to apply to our own marriages. We are beyond blessed for the ways they showed love for each other, the lessons they have taught us, and, the way they have loved and served the Lord. Our grandpa truly desired for the Lord's Will to be above all other matters in their lives, and sought to trust Him with deep faith and praise Him in return, no matter the outcome. We are truly grateful for Karl J. Feucht being our grandpa, and if you never had the chance to meet him, we hope someday you can sit down with him in heaven and listen as he tells a story from his childhood or shares a simple joke with a twinkle in his eye.

Karl and Elisabeth Feucht

October 2014

74743606R00095